Modeling Techniques with CINEMA 4D R17® Studio

The Ultimate Beginner's Guide

Team Rising Polygon

and

ROC

RISING POLYGON

Modeling Techniques with CINEMA 4D R17 Studio - The Ultimate Beginner's Guide

Copyright © 2016 Rising Polygon

Book Code: RPO3C

ISBN: 978-1533185297

Web: http://www.risingpolygon.co

Author Email: rconor@risingpolygon.co

e-Book Link: http://bit.ly/c4dmod

Contents

Acknowledgements

Thanks to:

Everyone at Maxon [**www.maxon.net**].
Everyone at Microsoft [**www.microsoft.com**].

Thanks to all great digital artists who inspire us with their innovative VFX, gaming, animation, and motion graphics content.

And a very special thanks to wonderful CG artists of London, UK.

Finally, thank you for picking up the book.

This page intentionally left blank

About the Author

Rising Polygon, founded by **Ravi Conor** aka **ROC**, and **Gordon Fisher** is a group of like-minded professionals and freelancers who are specialized in advertising, graphic design, web design and development, digital marketing, multimedia, exhibition, print design, branding, and CG content creation.

ROC has over a decade of experience in the computer graphics field and although he's primarily a shading and texturing artist, he's also experienced in the fields of Dynamics, UVMapping, Lighting, and Rendering. Along side 3D Studio Max, Ben's has experience with VRay, Maya, FumeFX, Mudbox, Mari, Photoshop, xNormal, UVLayout, Premiere, and After Effects.

You can contact **ROC** by sending an e-mail to author using the following Email ID: rconor@risingpolygon.co.

This page intentionally left blank

Preface

Why this Book?

The **Modeling Techniques with CINEMA 4D R17 Studio - The Ultimate Beginner's Guide** textbook offers a hands-on exercises based strategy for all those digital artists who have just started working on the CINEMA 4D [no experience needed] and interested in learning modeling in CINEMA 4D. This brilliant guide takes you step-by-step through the whole process of modeling. From the very first pages, the users of the book will learn how to effectively use CINEMA 4D for hard-surface modeling. A bonus chapter has been included in this edition containing six additional hands-on exercises.

What you need?

To complete the examples and hands-on exercises in this book, you need R17 Studio version of CINEMA 4D.

What are the main features of the book?

- The book is written using CINEMA 4D R17 Studio in an easy to understand language.
- Polygon and Spline modeling techniques covered.
- All deformers explained.
- 17 Hands-on exercises and 13 practical tests to hone your skills.
- Detailed coverage of tools and features.
- Additional tips, guidance, and advice is provided.
- Important terms are in bold face so that you never miss them.
- Support for technical aspect of the book.
- CINEMA 4D files and textures used are available for download from the accompanying website.
- Bonus hands-on exercises.

Is this book is available in e-Book format?

Yes. You can download e-Book from the following link: **http://bit.ly/c4dmod**.

How This Book Is Structured?

This book is divided into following units:

Unit CI2: Tools of the Trade

- Navigating the workspace
- Customizing the interface
- Understanding various UI components
- Setting preferences for CINEMA 4D
- Understanding layouts
- Moving, rotating, and scaling objects
- Managers, and Browsers
- Getting help

Unit CI2: Tools of the Trade

- Creating guides in the editor view
- Interactively placing lights and adjusting their attributes in the scene
- Measuring angles and distances
- Working with **Workplanes**
- Arranging, duplicating, and randomizing objects
- Correcting lens distortions
- Creating virtual walkthroughs

Unit CM1: Spline Modeling

- Splines tools and modeling techniques
- Generator command group

Unit CM2: Polygon Modeling

- Polygons components
- Polygon modeling techniques
- Selection tools
- Polygons structure tools
- Splines structure tools
- Modeling Objects
- Deformers

Unit CBEM1: Bonus Hands-on Exercises

Examination Copies

Books received as examination copies are for review purposes only and may not be made available for student use. Resale of the examination copies is prohibited. If you want to receive this book as an examination copy, send the request from your official e-mail id to us using the **Contact** page from our website.

Electronic Files

Any electronic file associated with this book are licensed to the original user only. These files can not be transferred to a third party. However, the original user can use these files in personal projects without taking any permission from **Rising Polygon**.

Trademarks

CINEMA 4D is the registered trademarks of **Maxon Computer**. **Windows** is the registered trademarks of **Microsoft Inc.**

Disclaimer

Access to Electronic Files

This book is sold via multiple sales channels. If you don't have access to the resources used in this book, you can place a request for the resources by visiting the following link: *http://bit.ly/resources-rp.*

Customer Support

At **Rising Polygon**, our technical team is always ready to take care of your technical queries. If you are facing any problem with the technical aspect of the book, navigate to *http://bit.ly/contact-rp* and let us know about your query.

Reader Feedback

Your feedback is always welcome. Your feedback is critical to our efforts at **Rising Polygon** and it will help us in developing quality titles in the future. To send the feedback, visit *http://bit.ly/contact-rp.*

Errata

We take every precaution while preparing the content of the book but mistakes do happen. If you find any mistake in this book general or technical, we would be happy that you report it to us so that we can mention it in the errata section of the book's online page. If you find any errata, please report them by visiting the following link: *http://bit.ly/contact-rp*. This will help the other readers from frustration. Once your errata is verified, it will appear in the errata section of the book's online page.

Contact Author

Stay connected with us through Twitter (**@risingpolygon**) to know the latest updates about our products, information about books, and other related information. You can also send an e-mail to author at the following address: **rconor@risingpolygon.co**.

Unit CI1: Introducing CINEMA 4D R17 Studio

Welcome to the latest version of CINEMA 4D. In any 3D computer graphics application, the first thing you encounter is interface. Interface is where you view and work with your scene. The CINEMA 4D's interface is intuitive and highly customizable. You can make changes to the interface and then save multiple interface settings using the **Layout** feature. You can create multiple layouts and switch between them easily.

In this unit, I'll describe the following:

- Navigating the workspace
- Customizing the interface
- Understanding various UI components
- Setting preferences for CINEMA 4D
- Understanding layouts
- Moving, rotating, and scaling objects
- Managers, and Browsers
- Getting help

CINEMA 4D Interface Elements

You can start CINEMA 4D by using one of the following methods:

- Double-click on the CINEMA 4D icon
- Double-click on a CINEMA 4D scene file
- Clicking CINEMA 4D entry from the **Start** menu
- Dragging a *.c4d* file from the explorer to the program icon
- Running it from the Command Prompt
- Running CINEMA 4D Lite from the After Effects

When you first time open CINEMA 4D, you are presented with the UI, as shown in Figure F1. I have labeled various elements of the interface using numbers. The following table summarizes the main UI elements.

Table 1: The CINEMA 4D Interface Elements Overview		
No.	Name	Description
1	Menubar	The menubar contains the most important CINEMA 4D commands and functions.
2	Standard Palette	It is located below the menubar. This palette [or toolbar] hosts tools, commands, and functions.

3	Tools Palette	This palette [or toolbar] contains most commonly used commands and tools.
4	Command Groups	The command groups are the collection of tools and commands.
5	Navigation Buttons	You can use these buttons to navigate a scene.
6	Layout drop-down	The options from this drop-down are used to switch between layouts.
7	Object Manager	This manager contains all objects of a scene.
8	Attribute Manager	It displays the properties and settings of the selected objects.
9	Coordinate Manager	It contains fields that you can use to precisely model and manipulate an object in the scene.
10	Material Manager	It contains all the materials for the scene.
11	Animation Toolbar	This toolbar contains controls for recording and playing animation.
12	Menu in editor view	This menu is available in every viewport and used to set various tasks related to the viewports. In the later chapters, I've referred to it as **MEV** menubar.
13	View Panel	The view panel is collection of upto four viewports where you build and animate 3D models.
14	Title Bar	The tile bar of the main window.

The CINEMA 4D interface is highly configurable. You can dock and undock windows from the main window. When you move a docked window, the surrounding windows are resized automatically. You can also display windows as tabs to save the screen real-state. You can define the arrangements of elements as layouts and freely switch between them. The fastest way to switch between the layouts is the **Layout** drop-down [labeled as 6 in Figure F1] located on the top-right corner of the interface.

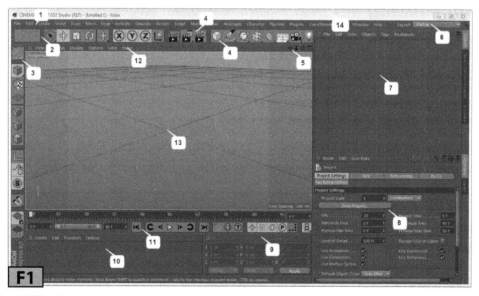

See Video: UCI1-01.mp4

Let's explore various components of the CINEMA 4D interface.

Title Bar

The title bar is the first element of the interface and located at the top of the UI. It displays name and version of the software as well as the currently opened file.

Menubar

The menubar is located below the tile bar. It hosts almost all important commands, tools, and functions that CINEMA 4D offer. You can tear-off a menu [or sub-menu] from the menubar by clicking on the double-line located at the top of the menu or sub-menu [see Figure F2].

Standard Palette

The **Standard** palette is located below the menubar and it hosts various tools, commands, and group of commands. Some of the icons on the palette have a black triangle on the bottom-right corner that indicates a folded group of commands.

To access these commands, press and hold the LMB on the icon and then choose the desired command from the displayed flyout. The following table summarizes the tools available in the **Standard** Palette:

F2

Name	Icon	Shortcut	Description
Undo		Ctrl+Z	This tools undoes the last change. It restores scene to the previous state. By default, you can restore up to **30** previous states. If you want to change the depth. Choose **Preferences** from the **Edit** menu to open the **Preferences** window. Choose **Memory** from the list of categories and then set a new value for the **Undo Depth** attribute in the **Project** group.
Redo		Ctrl+Y	This tool redoes a change. It restore the changes you made.
Live Selection		9	It is like a paint brush type of selection tool. To change the brush size, change the value of the **Radius** attribute in the **Attribute Editor**. To interactively change the radius, press and hold MMB and drag. To select entities, paint over the objects, points, edges, or polygons. You can quickly select the elements when the **Rotate, Move,** or **Scale** tool is active by RMB dragging over the objects. You can press **Spacebar** to toggle between the **Live Selection** tool and previously selected tool.

Table 2: The tools and commands available in the **Standard** palette

Rectangle Selection		O	This tool allows you to select the tools by dragging a selection frame [like marquee selection in Photoshop] over the elements. To add an element to the selection, hold **Shift** while you select. To deselect an element, hold **Ctrl** while you select.
Lasso Selection		8	This tool behaves like a lasso. You can use it to draw a loop around elements to select them.
Polygon Selection		-	This tools allows you to draw a n-sided shape to frame the elements to select them. To complete the loop, click on the starting point or RMB click. [*See Video: UCI1-02.mp4*]
Move Tool		E/4/7	Allows you to place the selected object or *component* in the viewport. You can also use it to select objects, points, edges, or polygons. The selection can also be drawn using the RMB. [*see Video: UCI1-03.mp4*]. You can also use the **Axis Extension** feature to accurately position the objects, *see Video: UCI1-04.mp4*. You can press the 4 key and drag the mouse to move the object. Press 7 and drag the mouse to move the objects without child objects.
Scale Tool		T	Allows you to resize the selected objects or components. **Axis Extension** function is also available for the **Scale** Tool.
Rotate Tool		R	Allows you to rotate the selected objects or components. For **Axis Extension**, see *Video: UCI1-05.mp4*.
Active Tool	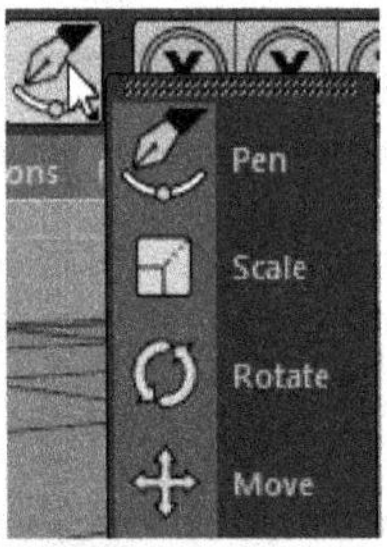		A list of last used 8 tools is displayed here when you click and hold on it.
X-Axis / Heading		X	This tool locks or unlocks the transformation along the X-axis, *see Video: UCI1-06.mp4*.
Y-Axis / Pitch		Y	This tool locks or unlocks the transformation along the Y-axis, *see Video: UCI1-06.mp4*.

Tool	Icon	Shortcut	Description
Z-Axis / Bank		Z	This tool locks or unlocks the transformation along the Z-axis, *see Video: UCI1-06.mp4*.
Coordinate System		W	This tool is a toggle switch that allows you to switch between the local and world coordinate systems, *see Video: UCI1-06.mp4*.
Render View		Ctrl+R	Renders the current active view.
Render to Picture Viewer		Shift+R	Renders the active view in the **Picture Viewer** window.
Edit Render Settings		Ctrl+B	Opens the **Render Settings** window from where you can specify settings for rendering the scene.
Cube			Click on the **Cube** tool to create a cube. Press and hold the LMB on this tool to reveal the **Objects** command group. This group holds all other primitives that CINEMA 4D offers.
Pen			This tool is a new entry in CINEMA 4D R17. It has replaced the old versions of the **Bézier, B-Spline, Linear** and **Akima Spline** tools. Press and hold the LMB on this tool to reveal the **Spline** command group. This group holds the spline primitives and other spline tools CINEMA 4D offers.
Subdivision Surface			This tool is generator that allows you to easily create 3D models with low poly count. This tool supports point weighting, edge weighting, and so forth. Press and hold LMB on this tool to reveal the **Generators** command group. This group holds the generators that CINEMA 4D offers.
Array			This tool creates copies of the objects and arranges them in a spherical form or wave form. Press and hold the LMB on this tool to reveal the **Modeling Objects** command group. This group holds various modeling commands.
Bend			This tool bends the objects. Press and hold the LMB on this tool to reveal the **Deformer** command group. This group holds the deformer functions CINEMA 4D offers.
Floor			This tool creates a floor object that always lies in the XZ plane of the world coordinate system. It stretches to infinity in all directions. Press and hold the LMB on this tool to reveal other environment tools available in the **Environment** command group.

Camera			This tool create a camera in the scene. Press and hold the LMB on this tool to reveal other camera tools available in the **Camera** command group.
Light			This tool create a light in the scene. Press and hold the LMB on this tool to reveal other light tools available in the **Light** command group.

Highlighting and Selections

The selected objects are surrounded by an orange outline. If you hover the mouse over objects in the editor view, a white outline appears on the objects underneath the mouse pointer. If you are using a graphics card that is not supported by CINEMA 4D, these highlights will not appear. In case you have a supported graphics card and highlights are not appearing, you need to turn on **Enhanced OpenGL**. You can access this option from the **Options** menu of the **Menu in editor view**.

Tools Palette

The Tools palette is the vertical toolbar located on the extreme left of the default interface. It contains various tools. The following table summarizes these tools:

Table 3: The tools and commands available in the **Tools** palette

Name	Icon	Shortcut	Description
Make Editable		C	The primitive objects in CINEMA 4D are parametric. They have no points or polygons and are instead created using math. This tool allows you to convert the parametric objects to editable objects with polygons and points. When you make an object editable, you lose its parametric creation parameters.
Model			If you want to move, rotate, or scale an object, use this mode.
Object			The **Object** mode is suited when you are working with an animation. When you scale an object using the **Scale** tool, only the object axes are scaled not the surfaces themselves. If you scale an object non-uniformly, the child objects get squashed and stretched when you rotate them. You can avoid this problem by working in the **Object** mode. The rule of thumb is when modeling, use the **Model** mode, use the **Object** mode for animation.
Texture			This mode allows you to edit the active texture. Only one texture can be edited at a time. Also, note that the projection type is also taken into consideration in this mode.
Workplane			Workplanes are explained in detail in Unit 2.
Points			Select this tool to enable point mode. Once enabled you can use edit the points of an object.

Edges			Click this tool to edit the edges of an object.
Polygons			Click this tool to edit polygons of an object.
Enable Axis		L	This tool allows you to move the origin of the object.
Tweak			This tool works with the **Polygon Pen** tool. You can tweak points, edges, and polygons using the **Polygon Pen** tool in this mode.
Viewport Solo Mode			This mode is useful when you are working on a complex scene and you want to concentrate on a specific area of the scene. The **Viewport Solo Off** is a toggle switch that you can use to turn on or off the **Viewport Solo** mode. In the **Viewport Solo Single** mode, all objects are hidden except the currently selected objects. The **Viewport Solo Hierarchy** mode displays on the selected objects, including their child objects.
Enable Snap		Shift+S	It is a toggle switch that lets you enable or disable snapping.
Locked Workplane		Shift+X	This tool disables any defined automatic **Workplane** modes and fixes the **Workplane**.
Planar Workplane			Depending on the angle of view of the camera, one of the world coordinate planes will be automatically displayed as the **Workplane**.

Navigation Tools

The navigation tools are located on the top-right corner of each viewport. Click-drag the first icon to pan the view [move the camera], click-drag second icon to zoom in or out [move the camera in the direction of view] of the viewport. Click-drag the third icon to rotate [rotate the camera] the view. Click the forth icon to maximize the view. You can also maximize a viewport by MMB clicking on it. You can also use the hotkeys to navigate the view. To use a hotkey, hold down the key on the keyboard and drag the mouse. The following table summarizes these hotkeys:

Table 4: The navigation hotkeys	
Key	**Description**
1	Move camera.
2	Move camera in the direction of view
3	Rotate Camera

The viewports with the orthogonal view can be rotated around their orthographic axis. If you hold **Shift**, you can rotate the camera in **15** degrees increments.

Menu In Editor View

The **Menu in editor view** [I will refer to it as **MEV** menubar now onwards] is located on the top of each viewport. It hosts command, tools, and functions corresponding to the views. The **MEV** menubar contains six menus.

The following tables summarizes the options available in these menus:

Table 5: The View menu

Option	Icon	Shortcut	Description
Use as Render View			When enabled, the active camera will be used for the rendering in the **Picture Viewer**.
Undo View/ Redo View		Ctrl+Shift+Z Ctrl+Shift+Y	These tools only work in the viewports. The main **Undo/Redo** tools do not affect the cameras.
Frame All			Centers all objects including lights and cameras to fill the view.
Frame Geometry		Alt+H H	Centers all objects excluding lights and cameras to fill the view.
Frame Default			Resets the viewport to the default values.
Frame Selected Elements		Alt+S S	Centers all selected elements [objects, polygons] to fill the view.
Frame Selected Objects		Alt+O O	Centers all active objects to fill the view.
Film Move/ Film Magnify/ Film Zoom			The functioning of these tools is similar to those of the navigation tools, refer to Table 4.
Redraw		A	Redraws the scene. By default, CINEMA 4D updates the scene automatically. If it does not happen, use this function to redraw the scene.

Table 6: The **Camera** menu

Option	Icon	Description
Cursor Mode		Every viewport has a default camera called the **Editor Camera**. This camera is active by default. These modes define how camera is rotated. If you have defined a camera and using it, it will be always rotated around its origin independent of the **Camera Mode**. The **Cursor** mode is the default mode. In this mode the camera rotates around the selected object point. If you click on an empty area of the viewport, the camera will pivot around that point.
Center Mode		In this mode, the camera will rotate around the screen center.
Object Mode		In this mode, the camera will rotate around the center of the selected objects/elements
Camera Mode		In this mode, the camera will rotate around its own axis.
Default Camera		The command activates the default camera.
Set Active Object as Camera		You can use this function to view the scene from the origin of the active object.
Perspective		This is the default projection mode for the viewport [see Figure F3]. You see the scene as if you are looking through a conventional camera.
Parallel		All lines are parallel. The vanishing point is infinitely distant [see Figure F4].
Left		The YZ view [see Figure F5].
Right		The ZY view [see Figure F6].
Front		The XY view [see Figure F7].
Back		The YX view [see Figure F8].

Top	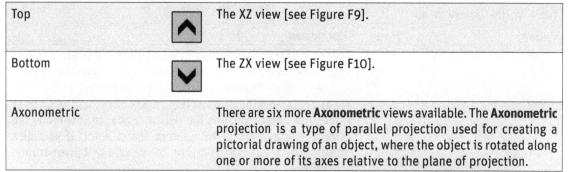	The XZ view [see Figure F9].
Bottom		The ZX view [see Figure F10].
Axonometric		There are six more **Axonometric** views available. The **Axonometric** projection is a type of parallel projection used for creating a pictorial drawing of an object, where the object is rotated along one or more of its axes relative to the plane of projection.

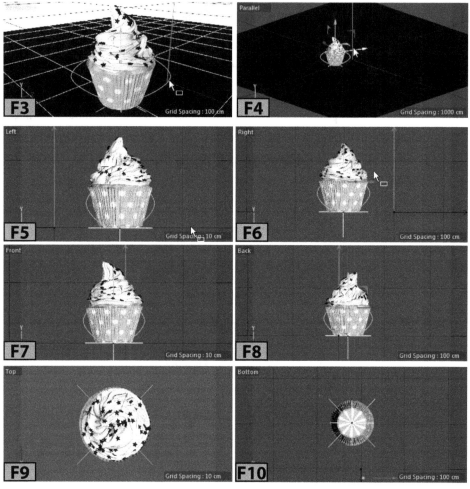

Table 7: The **Display** menu			
Option	**Icon**	**Shortcut**	**Description**
Gouraud Shading	⚪	N~A	This is the high quality display mode for viewports [see Figure F11]. The object smoothing and lights are taken into consideration.

Gouraud Shading (Lines)		N~B	Adds wireframes or isoparms to the shading [see Figure F12].
Quick Shading		N~C	Identical to the **Gouraud Shading**, however, the auto light is used instead of scene's lights.
Quick Shading (Lines)		N~D	In this mode, you can add wireframes or isoparms to the quick shading by choosing **Wireframe** or **Isoparms** from the **Display** menu.
Constant Shading		N~E	Shows constant shading on the objects.
Constant Shading (Lines)			Shows constant shading with lines on the objects.
Hidden Line		N~F	The hidden lines are not displayed.
Lines		N~G	Displays complete mesh including hidden lines.
Wireframe		N~H	Draws lines on objects.
Isoparms		N~I	This mode displays isoparm lines for objects that use them such as **Generator** objects.
Box		N~K	Displays each object as box.
Skeleton		N~L	This is the fastest display mode. It is only suitable for hierarchical structures.

F11

Grid Spacing : 100 cm

F12

Table 8: The **Options** menu

Option	Icon	Shortcut	Description
[Level of Detail] Low Medium High			These options define level of detail in the viewport. The **Low**, **Medium**, and **High** options set the level of detail in the viewport to **25%**, **50%**, and **100%**, respectively.
Use Render LOD for Editor Rendering			Using this option, you can define LOD detail for each view. This option lets you use the LOD settings defined in the respective settings such as subdivision surfaces or metaballs.
Stereoscopic			Enables the stereoscopic display in the view.
Linear Workflow Shading			If you are considering a stereoscopic view, the color and shaders can be turned off using this option.
Enhanced OpenGL			Defines whether the viewport should use the **Enhanced OpenGL** quality for display.
Transparency			Defines whether or not **Enhanced OpenGL** should display transparency in high quality.
Shadows			Defines whether or not **Enhanced OpenGL** should display shadows.
Post Effects			Defines whether or not **Enhanced OpenGL** should display post effects.
Noises			Toggles the display of the **Noise** shader for **Enhanced OpenGL**.
Backface Culling		N~P	Toggles backface culling on or off when in the **Lines** mode. With backface culling, all concealed surfaces are hidden from the camera improving the performance.
Isoline Editing		Alt+A	It projects all Subdivision Surfaces cage object elements onto the smoothed surface. As a result, these elements can be selected directly on the smoothed object.

Layer Color			This option lets you view which objects have been assigned to which layer. The objects are displayed in the color assigned to their respective layer.
Normals			Toggles the display of normals in the polygon mode.
Tags		N~O	If enabled, the objects will use the display mode defined in their Display tags.
Textures		N~Q	Allows you to see textures in the view panel in real-time.
X-Ray		N~R	Enables the X-Ray effect. The object becomes semi-transparent so that you can see its concealed points and faces.
DefaultLight			Opens the Default Light manager that you can use to quickly light the selected objects.
Configure		Shift+V	The **Configure** option is used to specify the viewport settings. The settings are displayed in the **Attribute Manager**. The options and parameters displayed in bold in the **Attribute Manager** are saved globally and these options are used when you create a new scene or restart CINEMA 4D. All non-bold parameters and options are saved with the file locally. The local options and parameters affect the active view or the selected view. You can select multiple views by clicking on the blank gray area of their headers with **Shift** held down. You can make an option or a parameter global or local. To do this, select the element by clicking on it in the **Attribute Manager** and then RMB click. Choose **Make Parameter Global/Make Parameter Local** from the popup menu.
Configure All		Alt+V	This option affects all existing views.

The options in the **Filter** menu allow you to define which types of objects are displayed in the views. By default, all types are displayed. Choose **All** from the menu to enable all types. Choose **None** to disable all types.

Tip: Filters
*To enable one option and disable all others, choose the desired Filter from the **Filter** menu with **Ctrl** held down.*

Note: Hidden Objects
*If you select a hidden object from the **Object Manager**, the axis system of the object appears in the viewport.*

Each view panel in CINEMA 4D can have upto four view panels. The options available in the **Panel** menu allow you to choose a different mode [arrangement of viewports] for the view panel. Figure F13 shows the viewport arrangement when I chose **Arrangement | Views Top Split** from the **Panel** menu.

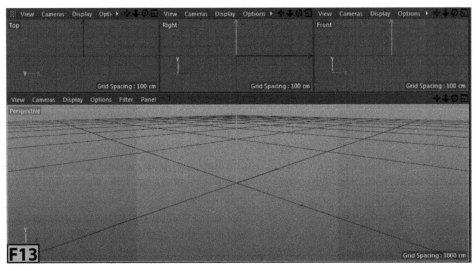

You can use the Function keys to toggle between the full-screen and normal size. You can also access the corresponding functions from the **Panel** menu. The following table summarizes these keys:

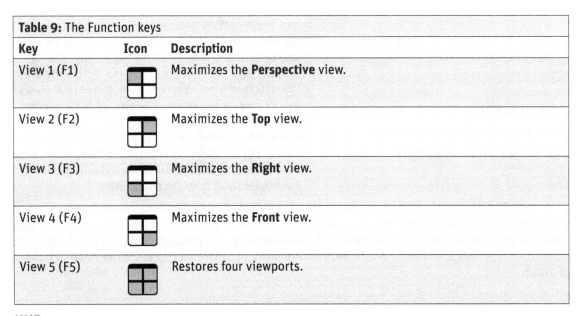

Key	Icon	Description
View 1 (F1)		Maximizes the **Perspective** view.
View 2 (F2)		Maximizes the **Top** view.
View 3 (F3)		Maximizes the **Right** view.
View 4 (F4)		Maximizes the **Front** view.
View 5 (F5)		Restores four viewports.

Table 9: The Function keys

HUD

The term HUD is taken from the aviation industry. In aircraft, HUD refers to the projection of reading on a screen so that the pilot can read the values without looking down. HUD in CINEMA 4D does the same function. The HUD can be switched on and off from the **Filter** page of the **Viewport** settings. To access this page, choose **Configure** from the **EV's Options** menu. *See Video: UCI1-07.mp4*

There are variety of managers, explorers, and browsers that CINEMA 4D offers. Here's the quick rundown:

Object Manager

Object Manager is the nerve center for all objects and their corresponding tags in a scene. This manager allows you to manage object's name, hierarchy, visibility, and so forth. It also allows you to manage tags that have been assigned to the objects.

Here're the few functions of the **Object Manager**:

- To select an object, click on it. To select multiple objects, click with **Ctrl** held down. You can use **Shift** to select an entire range of objects. You can also select multiple objects by holding down **Shift** and using the **Up** and **Down** arrow keys. The objects can also be selected by drawing a marquee selection. When you select an object, its settings are displayed in the **Attribute Manger**. When you select multiple objects, common settings are displayed in the **Attribute Manager**.
- MMB click selected an object including all its children.
- Alt+MMB click selects the object you click and all objects on the same hierarchy level except children.
- The selected items are color highlighted. The last selected object highlighted in slightly lighter color. Child objects of the selected objects are also highlighted in a lighter color.
- To open and close branches in the **Object Manager**, click + or - sign. If you want to open or close the entire hierarchy, click + or - sign with the **Ctrl** held down.
- Press the left or right arrow key to close or open the active branches.
- To make copies of an object, drag it with **Ctrl** held down.
- You can rearrange items in the manager by dragging and dropping.
- To rename items, double-click on their names. You can also select an item and press **Enter** to enable a rename field in which you can type the new name. When rename field appears, you can use the up and down arrow keys to quickly rename the items.
- The second column in the **Object Manager** [see Figure F14] contains some switches labeled from 1 to 4 in Figure 14 [sometimes also referred to as **Traffic Lights**]. The **Layer color** switch, labeled as 1, displayed the color of the layer. Click on this switch to open a popup menu. You can add the object to a layer or open the **Layer Manager** to have a greater controls on layers and objects they host.

- The switch labeled as 2, is the **Editor On/Off** switch. It allows you to control the visibility of the object in the editor view. By default, the color of this switch is gray, which is the default behavior. Click on it to override the default behavior and turn the visibility of the object on. The color of the switch turns green. Click one more time to hide the object from the editor view. On doing so, the color of the switch turns red. The green dot enforces the visibility of an object. If you have grouped several objects [Hotkey: **Alt+G**] and now you turn off the visibility of the group using red dots, you can still make the objects visible from the group by using the green dots.
- The switch labeled as 3, allows you to visibility of the objects in renders.

- The switch labeled as 4, affects the object in the editor view as well as in renderer. It essentially a way to turn off an object completely.
- The right side of the switches column is the area where you will find the tags associated with the objects.

Rearranging Objects

There are many ways for rearranging objects in the **Object Manager**. When you drag the objects, different icons appears on the mouse pointer indicating what action CINEMA 4D will take once you drop them. The following table summarizes these icons.

Table 10: Rearranging Objects	
Icon	**Description**
	Drag an object between two others or to the end of the list.
	Ctrl+Drag to create a copy.
	Makes the dragged object a child of the other.
	Use **Ctrl-drag** and move the mouse pointer over an object to create a copy and make it a child of another object.
	You can also drag-and-drop tags. To transfer a tag from one object to another, drag the tag icon on to the line of the other object.
	If you want to create a copy, use **Ctrl+Drag**.
	No operation is available.

Attribute Manager

The **Attribute Manager** allows you to specify value for almost every parameters in CINEMA 4D. You can access parameters of objects, tools, materials, and so forth from this manager. You can also animate parameters in the **Attribute Manager**. By default, it displays attributes the selected object. If you are using an object frequently, you can create a copy of the **Attribute Manager** and then lock it to that object. To create a new manager, click on the + icon [⊞] located on the top-right corner of the title bar. To lock the manager, click the lock icon [🔒] on the manager's title bar.

Coordinate Manager

The **Coordinate Manager** allows you to manipulate objects numerically. It displays fields for editing position, scale, and rotation values. You can also use it as a reference when you are scaling objects interactively in the editor view. The values are displayed in conjunction with the tool you are using. For example, if you are using the **Move Tool**, the position, size, and rotation values of the selected element are shown in the fields.

Note: Scaling Objects
*Scale the objects only when there is no other way. For example, if you want to make a sphere bigger, use its **Radius** attributes instead of scaling it up. Also, see the **Object** mode description in Table 3.*

Material Manager

The **Material Manager** allows you to create materials and apply them onto the objects in the scene. The thumbnail of each material you create is displayed in the manager. When you select an object in the **Object Manager**, the thumbnails of the materials applied to that object appear depressed. To apply a material to an object, drag the material's thumbnail from the **Material Manager** and drop it on an object(s) in the **Attribute Manager** or in the editor view.

Take Manager

When you are working on a complex project that contains various animations, render settings, cameras, and so forth, you will have to prepare and maintain several project files. Working on different files wastes a lot of time and effort. The **Take Manager** [see Figure F15] allows you to overcome this issue by saving multiple settings in one file and then can be rendered with powerful variable file and path names (**Tokens**). The **Take Manager** lets you save the initial state as the master take and then you can create new animations to fine-tune and test the scene.

Content Browser

The **Content Browser** [see Figure F16] allows you to navigate through the content libraries that come with CINEMA 4D. You can easily import the additional content and presets into your projects. You can use this manager to manage scenes, images, materials, shaders, and presets. This browser lets you manage file structure of your scene.

Structure Manager

The **Structure Manager** [see Figure F17] shows the data related to an object if the selected object is editable. This manager shows data like a spreadsheet. It contains cells that are divided into rows and columns. The data shown in the cells depends on the mode you are in. The following data is shown in the **Structure Manager**:

- Points
- Polygons
- UVW Coordinates
- Bezier Spline Tangents
- Weight Vertices
- Normal Vector Coordinates

The values shown in the cells can be directly edited. You can also drag and drop the lines. The editing functions such as cut, copy, and paste are also supported.

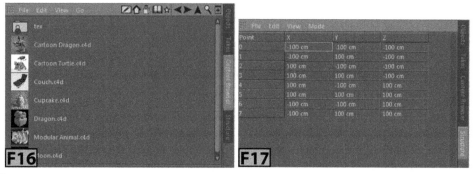

Layer Manager

The **Layer Manager** [see Figure F18] displays all layers that you have created. It is very useful when you are working on a complex scene. It lets you manage a complex scene easily. You can assign a custom color to the layer that also appears in the **Object Manager**. You can drag and drop a layer onto an object to assign that object to the dragged layer. If you hold down the **Ctrl/Cmd** key while dragging and dropping a layer onto an item, the layer is assigned to the item's children as well.

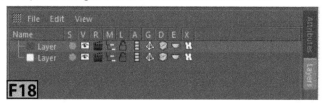

Project Settings

You can use the **Project Settings** [see Figure F19] to define standard values such as animation time, scene scale, and so forth for the current scene. These are the settings that affect the scene globally. You can open **Project Settings** by choosing **Project Settings** from the **Edit** menu. You can also open it by choosing **Mode | Project** from the **Attribute Manager** menu bar.

Help

The CINEMA 4D help documentation can be accessed by choosing **Help** from the **Help** menu. Like any other window in CINEMA 4D, the help window can be docked anywhere in the interface. CINEMA 4D also supports context sensitive help. If you want to access help for a button, tool, icon, and so forth, hover the mouse pointer on the element and then press **Ctrl+F1**. You can also RMB click on an attribute and then choose Show Help from the popup menu to see help documentation about that attribute.

If you hover the mouse pointer over almost any item in CINEMA 4D, a brief description about the item appears in the bottom-most window of the interface.

Commander

The **Commander** window in CINEMA 4D is used to call up commands, objects, tools, and tags without using any manager. You can invoke the **Commander** window by clicking on the magnifying glass icon located next to the **Layout** drop-down in the top-left corner of the interface.

Alternatively, you can press **Shift+C** to open it. Type the name of the entity you are looking for; CINEMA 4D will display a list of matching commands [see Figure F20]. Select the desired option from the list. You can press **ESC** to close the **Commander** window.

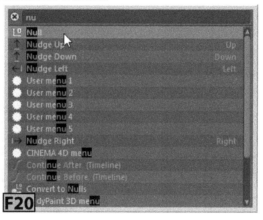

Hidden Menus

There are several hidden menus available in CINEMA 4D. These menus quickly allow you to select tools, command, and functions. The **V** menu [see Figure F21] provides a useful shortcut to quickly switch between the view, selection, tools/modes, plugins, and snapping options.

The **M** menu [see Figure F22] lets you quickly access the modeling tools. For example, if you want to invoke the **Extrude** function, press **M+T**. The **N** menu [see Figure F23A] clones the options from the **Display** menu of the editor's menubar. The **P** menu allows you to access snapping functions and commands [see Figure F23B].

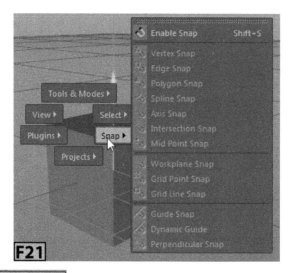

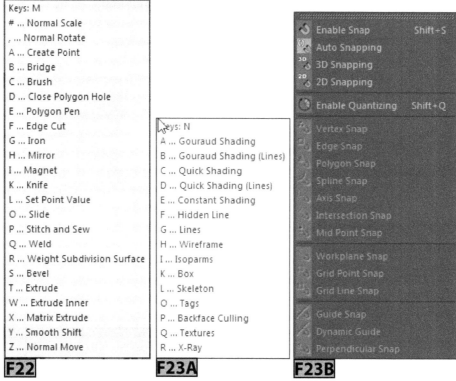

Keys: M

... Normal Scale
, ... Normal Rotate
A ... Create Point
B ... Bridge
C ... Brush
D ... Close Polygon Hole
E ... Polygon Pen
F ... Edge Cut
G ... Iron
H ... Mirror
I ... Magnet
K ... Knife
L ... Set Point Value
O ... Slide
P ... Stitch and Sew
Q ... Weld
R ... Weight Subdivision Surface
S ... Bevel
T ... Extrude
W ... Extrude Inner
X ... Matrix Extrude
Y ... Smooth Shift
Z ... Normal Move

F22

Keys: N

A ... Gouraud Shading
B ... Gouraud Shading (Lines)
C ... Quick Shading
D ... Quick Shading (Lines)
E ... Constant Shading
F ... Hidden Line
G ... Lines
H ... Wireframe
I ... Isoparms
K ... Box
L ... Skeleton
O ... Tags
P ... Backface Culling
Q ... Textures
R ... X-Ray

F23A

F23B

Hands-on Exercises

Before you start the hands-on exercises, let's first create a project folder that will host the exercise files. Open the **Windows Explorer** and create a new directory with the name **c4dr17studio** in the **C** drive of your system. Create a sub-folder with the name **unit-ci1** in the **c4dr17studio** folder.

Exercise 1: Creating a Sofa

In this exercise, you will model a sofa using the **Box** primitive [see Figure E1].

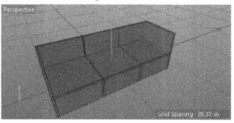

The following table summarizes the exercise:

Table E1: Creating Model of a Sofa	
Skill level	Beginner
Time to complete	30 Minutes
Topics in the section	• Getting Your Feet Wet • Creating One Seat Section of the Sofa • Creating Corner Section of the Sofa
Project Folder	c4dr17studio/unit-ci1
Units	Inches
Final exercise file	uci1-hoe1-end.c4d

Getting Your Feet Wet

Choose **File | New** from the main menubar or press **Ctrl+N** to start a new scene. Choose **Object | Cube** from the **Create** menu to create a cube at the center of the **Perspective** view. Ensure any selection tool is active in the **Standard** palette and then click and drag the green handle [along +Y-axis]. Notice that the new **Y** position value is displayed in the **Coordinate Manager** and **Status Bar** at the bottom of the UI [see Figure E2]. In the **Coordinate Manager | Position [Y]** field, enter **0** to place the cube back at the origin.

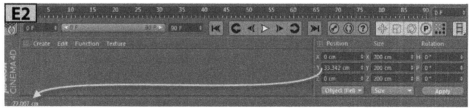

Choose **World** from the drop-down located below the **Position** fields in the **Coordinate Manager** and then enter **100** in the **Position [Y]** field. The cube now sits on the grid in the editor view. In the **Object Manager**, double-click on **Cube** and rename it as **myCube**. Notice the name is displayed in the **Attribute Manager** as well. In the **Attribute Manager**, ensure **Coord** parameter group is selected [see Figure E3] and then in **Freeze Transformation** section, click **Freeze P**.

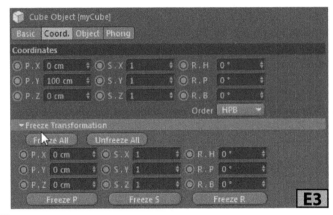

What just happened?

*Freezing transformations in CINEMA 4D freezes [zero out, also referred to as dual transformation] the coordinates of all selected objects. When you freeze coordinates, the local position and rotation coordinates will each be set to **0** and scale to **1** without changing position or orientation of the object. Freezing transformations is particularly useful in animations using parent–child relationships. When you rotate a child object around an axis, all three axes are affected because the parent object's coordinate system has a different orientation from the local coordinates. You can avoid this scenario by freezing the coordinates before animating.*

Tip: Parameter Groups

*The parameters of an objects are categorized in different groups in the **Attribute Manager**. Notice in Figure E3 there are four groups: **Basic**, **Coord**, **Object**, and **Phong**. The selected group button appears in the light blue color [**Coord** in this case]. If you want to display parameters from different groups in the **Attribute Manager**. Click on the parameter buttons with **Shift** or **Ctrl** held down. You can also click-drag on the buttons to display parameters from different groups.*

Choose **Object (Rel)** from the first drop-down in the **Coordinate Manager** and then enter **50** in the **Position [Y]** field. Notice now the cube moves **50** units up from its current position. **Object (Rel)** defines the relative object location without frozen coordinates. This is same as the main coordinates in the **Coord** parameter group of the **Attribute Manager**. **Object (Abs)** defines the relative object location as a combination of frozen coordinates and **Object (Rel)** coordinates. **World** defines the object location in world units.

In the **Object Manager**, drag **myCube** with **Ctrl** held down to create a copy of the cube with the name **myCube.1**. In the editor view, drag the green handle in the positive Y-axis to display both cubes [see Figure E4].

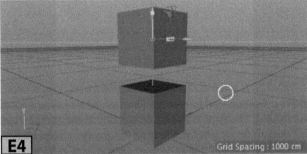

Drag **myCube.1** onto the **myCube** and release the mouse button when an icon similar to the one shown in Figure E5 to make **myCube.1** child of **myCube** [see Figure E6].

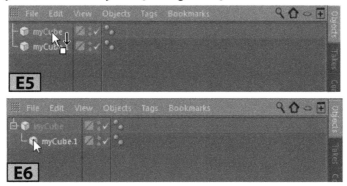

Choose **Size+** from the middle drop-down in the **Coordinate Manager**. Notice that the size of the parent+child is displayed in the **Scale** fields.

What just happened?

*The middle drop-down in the **Coordinate Manager** specifies which object size is shown in the Scale [XYZ] fields. **Size** shows the size of the object without considering children [see Figure E7] whereas **Size+** considers the children as well [see Figure E8]. **Scale** shows the axis length of the object coordinate system. Default value is **1:1:1** [see Figure E9].*

Note: Scale and Parent-child Relationship

*When you create a child of a parent, the scale of the child axis adjusted according to the parent so that the child appears normal with respect to the world axes. For example, if scale of the parent object is **4:1:1** and when you create a child for this object, the scale of the child axes will be **0.25:1:1**.*

Choose **Close** from the **File** menu or press **Ctrl+F4** to close the scene. Do not save the file.

Now, we understood the coordinate system therefore now let's move ahead and build the sofa. Before we jump into modeling, let's first set the units for the project.

Specifying Units

You can define units for the project from two locations in CINEMA 4D: **Preferences** window and **Project Settings**. Choose **Preferences** from the **Edit** menu or press **Ctrl+E**. Choose **Units** from the list of categories and then choose **Inches** from the **Unit Display** drop-down of **Basic** section. Close the **Preferences** window.

What just happened?

*Here, I chose **Inches** as units for the project. This setting does not affect the scene parameters [scale]. It just convert the values in the fields. For example, if you have defined a value of **20 cm** and you switch units to **Meters**, the filed will display the value **0.2m**. However, if you want to change the scale of the scene, you can do so from the **Project Settings** by adjusting the **Project Scale** parameter. If you change units to meters, a **20cm** wide object will be scaled to **20m** wide object.*

*You can open **Project Settings** in the **Attribute Manager** by choosing **Project Settings** from the **Edit** menu, or press **Ctrl+D**. To change scale of the scene, click **Scale Project** from the **Attribute Manager** to open the **Scale Project** dialog. In this dialog, set the **Target Scale** and then click **OK** to change the scale. This feature is specifically useful when you are importing an object created in an external application and does not have a correct scale.*

Press **Ctrl+S**, the **Save File** dialog appears. Navigate to the **\c4dr14studio\unit-i1** folder and save the file with the name **ui1-hoe1-end.c4d**.

*I highly recommend that you save your work at regularly by pressing **Ctrl+S**.*

Creating One Seat Section of the Sofa

On the **Standard** palette, click **Cube** 🔲 to create a cube in the editor view. On the **Attribute Manager** | **Object** parameter group, enter **25.591, 1**, and **25.591** in the **Size X**, **Size Y**, and **Size Z** fields, respectively. Press **Alt+O** to frame the cube in the editor view. Press **NB** to enable **Gouraud Shading (Lines)** display mode [see Figure E10]. Create another cube and then set cube's **Size X**, **Size Y**, and **Size Z** fields to **25.591**, **11.417**, and **1**, respectively.

Press **Ctrl+A** to select both the cubes. Choose **Arrange Objects** | **Center** from the **Tools** menu. On the **Attribute Manager** | **Options** parameter group, choose **Middle** and **Negative** from the **X Axis** and **Z Axis** drop-downs, respectively. Click **Apply** on the **Tool** parameter group to align objects [see Figure E11]. On the **Tool** parameter group, click **New Transform** and then choose **None, Positive, None** from the **X Axis**, **Y Axis**, and **Z Axis** drop-downs, respectively to align the two objects [see Figure E12]. Select **Cube.1** from the **Object Manager** or in the editor view and then align it with the bottom face of the cube using the **Move Tool** [see Figure E13]. You can switch to the **Right** viewport to align the cubes accurately.

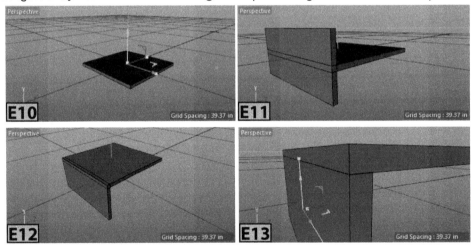

Make sure **Cube.1** is selected and then choose **Arrange Objects** | **Duplicate** from the **Tools** menu. In the **Attribute Manager** | **Duplicate** parameter group, enter **1** in the **Copies** field to create one duplicate of the cube. Choose **Linear** from the **Mode** drop-down in the **Options** parameter group. On the **Position** section, turn off the **X** and **Y** switches. Enter **24.5** in the **Move [Z]** field to move the duplicate on the other side [see Figure E14].

Now, we need to create the back support for the seat. Create another cube in the editor view and then set its **Size X**, **Size Y**, and **Size Z** fields to **1**, **25.591**, and **25.591**, respectively. Align the cube to the back of the seat using the process described above [see Figure E15]. Similarly, create a cube for the font section and align it [see Figure E16].

Hint: Aligning Objects

*Align **Cube.1** and **Cube.2** using the **Center** function along the negative x-axis.*

Press **Ctrl+A** to select all objects and then choose **Objects | Group Objects** from the **Attribute Editor's** menu. You can also press **Alt+G** to group the objects. Double-click on **Null** and rename it as **oneSeat**.

What just happened?

*Here, I've grouped objects [all cubes] in the **Attribute Manager**. A **Null** object is created and selected objects are placed inside the **Null**. Groups help you in better organizing your scene and keep the **Object Manager** neat and tidy. When you group objects with children, chid objects are also placed inside **Null** and object hierarchies are maintained. You can expand a group using the **Shift+G** hotkeys. The objects that are one level below the parent are moved to the same level as the parent and the existing hierarchies are preserved.*

Creating Corner Section of the Sofa

Here, we are going to create the corner seat for the sofa. Make sure **oneSeat** is selected and then create a copy of **oneSeat** in **Attribute Manager** or editor view [see Figure E17]. Rename the new group **Null** as **cornerSeat** in the **Object Manager**. On the **Object Manager**, select **cornerSeat | Cube.1_copies | Cube.1.0**. On the **Attribute Manager | Object** parameter group of **Cube.1.0**, set **Size X** and **Size Y** to **26.691** and **25.591**, respectively. Now, align the cube [see Figure E18]. Similarly, create **cornerSeat** for the other end [see Figure E19].

Hint: Corner Seat

*Create a copy of **cornerSeat** in **Attribute Manager** or editor view and then align it on the left of the **oneSeat**.*

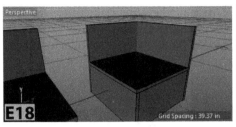 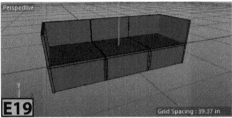

Exercise 2: Creating a Coffee Table

In this exercise, you will model a coffee table using the Cylinder and Torus primitives [see Figure E1].

The following table summarizes the exercise:

Table E2: Creating Model of a Coffee Table	
Skill level	Beginner
Time to complete	30 Minutes
Topics in the section	• Getting Started • Creating the Coffee Table
Project Folder	c4dr17studio/unit-ci1
Units	Inches
Final exercise file	uci1-hoe2-end.c4d

Getting Started

Start a new scene in CINEMA 4D and set units to Inches.

Note: Naming Terminology

Now onwards, I will be using the following terminologies for various interface entities:

AM - Attribute Manager, CM - Coordinate Manager, OM - Object Manager, MM - Material Manager, CB - Content Browser, PG - Parameter Group, SP - Standard Palette, LM - Layers Manager, CG - Command Group, and MEV - Menu in editor view .

Creating the Coffee Table

Press and hold the LMB on **Cube** 🔷 on **SP** and then click **Cylinder** 🛢 . Press **NB** to enable **Gouraud Shading (Lines)** display mode. On **AM | Cylinder | Object PG**, set **Radius**, **Height**, and **Rotation Segments** to **37.5**, **2**, and **60**, respectively.

Press and hold the LMB on **Cube** 🔲 on **SP** and then click **Torus** ⊙. On **AM** | **Torus** | **Object PG**, set **Ring Radius**, **Ring Segments**, **Pipe Radius** to **37.5**, **60**, and **1.521**, respectively. Align the two objects [see Figure E2]. Press **Alt+G** to group the two objects and rename the group's **Null** to **tableTop**.

Now, we will create a clone of **tableTop** to create the bottom part of the table. Invoke the **Move Tool** ✛ and ensure that **tableTop** is selected. Choose **Enable Quantizing** from the **Snap** menu or press **Shift+Q**. Drag the green Y-axis handle about **30** units in positive Y direction with **Ctrl** held down. To enter accurate value, enter **30** in the **Position [Y]** field of **CM** [see Figure E3]. In **OM**, rename the group as **tableBottom**. Press **Shift+Q** to disable the quantizing function.

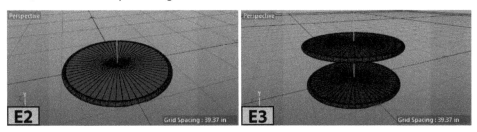

What just happened?
I have used the quantizing function. This function restricts stepless movement to a defined grid. For example, instead of a stepless rotation, you can allow rotation on 45 degrees increment. This function is primarily intended to use with the Move ✛ *, Scale* ⬚ *, and Rotate* ⟳ *tools. However, you can use it with other tools such as Polygon Pen* ✎ *. The following settings can also be included as GUI elements in Palettes for setting the step size [See Video: U1-V013-08.mp4].*

You can also access these settings from AM. Choose Modeling from AM's Mode menu to open the Modeling Settings. Now, select the Quantize PG to display the settings.

Press and hold the LMB on **Cube** 🔲 on **SP** and then click **Cylinder** ⬚ . Rename the cylinder as **leg**. On **AM** | **leg** | **Object PG**, set **Radius**, and **Height** to **2** and **50**, respectively. On **CM**, set **Position [Y]** and **Position [Z]** fields to **10**, and **40**, respectively to align leg with the **tableBottom** and **tableTop** [see Figure E4].

Now, its time to create two more copies of the leg. Ensure leg is selected in **OM** and then **Alt+click** on **Array** on **SP** to add an **Array** 🌐 object. By default, the **Array** object creates **7** copies [see Figure E5]. Also notice that the **Array** object has used center of leg as a pivot to arrange the copies. Now, we will fix it.

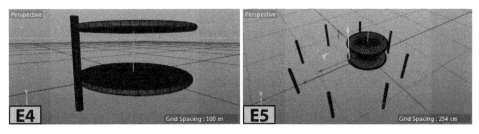

What just happened?
If you press Alt while selecting an object from SP, the selected object will become child of the new object. Otherwise, both object will be at the same level in AM.

On **AM | Array | Coord PG**, set **P Z** to **O**. On the **AM | Array | Object PG**, set **Copies** and **Radius** to **2**, and **40.5**, respectively.

Exercise 3: Creating a Foot Stool

In this exercise, you will model a foot stool using the Cube and Cylinder primitives [see Figure E1].

The following table summarizes the exercise:

Table E3: Creating Model of a Foot Stool	
Skill level	Beginner
Time to complete	30 Minutes
Topics in the section	• Getting Started • Creating a Foot Stool
Project Folder	c4dr17studio/unit-ci1
Units	Inches
Final exercise file	uci1-hoe3-end.c4d

Getting Started

Start a new scene in CINEMA 4D and set units to **Inches**.

Creating a Foot Stool

Press **NB** to enable the **Gouraud Shading (Lines)** mode. Click **Cube** ⬜ on the **Object** command group to add a cube to the editor view. Rename **Cube** as **baseGeo**. On **AM | baseGeo | Object PG**, set **Size X**, **Size Y**, and **Size Z** to **31.5**, **5**, and **24.8**, respectively. Turn on the **Fillet** switch and set **Fillet Radius** and **Fillet Subdivision** to **0.2** and **3**, respectively [see Figure E2].

Create another copy of the **baseGeo** by **Ctrl** dragging. Rename it as **topGeo** and place it on top of **baseGeo** [see Figure E3]. Select **topGeo** and on **AM | topGeo | Object PG**, set **Size Y** to **8**. Align the two objects [see Figure E4].

Now, we will create legs for the foot stool. Click **Cylinder** ⬜ on the **Object** command group to add a cylinder in the editor view. Rename it as **legGeo**. On **AM | legGeo | Object PG**, set **Radius** and **Height** to **1.5** and **4**, respectively. On **AM | legGeo | Caps PG**, turn on the **Fillet** switch and then set **Segments** and **Radius** to **3** and **0.5**, respectively. Align, **legGeo** with **baseGeo** [see Figure E5]. Create three more copies of **legGeo** and align them.

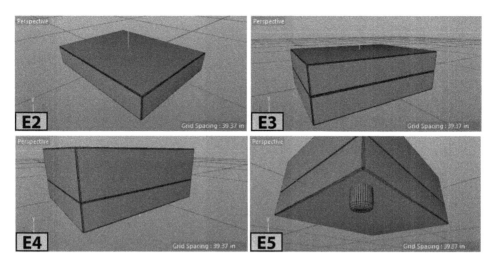

Let's now arrange objects in layers. Click **Layer** switch on the right of the **topGeo** and choose **Add to New Layer** [see Figure E6] from the popup menu; a new layer is created with the name **Layer** and **topGeo** is added to it. Also, CINEMA 4D assigns a color to the layer. Press **Shift+F4** to open the **LM**. On **LM**, double-click on **Layer** and rename it as **mainGeoLayer**. Drag **baseGeo** from **OM** to the **mainGeoLayer** layer on the **LM**. The **baseGeo** is now part of the layer **mainGeoLayer**.

Choose **File | New Layer** from the **LM's** menubar and rename the new layer as **legGeoLayer** [see Figure E7]. Drag **legGeoLayer** from **LM** to the **legGeo** in the editor view to make **legGeo** part of the layer. Notice that the color of layers is now reflected in the editor view which helps in identifying which object is part which layer. Now, drag **legGeoLayer** on **legGeo.1**, **legGeo.2**, and **legGeo.3**. Double-click on the color swatches in the **LM** to change the color of the layers.

There are many toggle switches on right of the layer name. The following table summarizes these switches:

Table E3.1: The **LM** toggle switches	
Icon	**Description**
S	Solo objects.
V	Visible in editor
R	Visible in render
M	Show in managers
L	Lock layer
A	Animation on/off
G	Generators on/off

D	Deformers on/off
E	Switches XPresso, C.O.F.F.E.E. tags, etc. on or off.
X	Update/load XRefs

Exercise 4: Creating a Bar Table

In this exercise, you will model a bar table using the **Cube** and **Cylinder** primitives [See Figure E1].

The following table summarizes the exercise:

Table E4: Creating a Bar Table	
Skill level	Beginner
Time to complete	30 Minutes
Topics in the section	• Getting Started • Creating a Bar Table
Project Folder	c4dr17studio/unit-ci1
Units	Inches
Final exercise file	uci1-hoe4-end.c4d

Getting Started

Start a new scene in CINEMA 4D and set units to **Inches**.

Creating a Foot Stool

Press **NB** to enable the **Gouraud Shading (Lines)** mode. Click **Cylinder** on the **Object** command group to add a cylinder in the editor view. Rename it as **topGeo**. On **AM | topGeo | Object PG**, set **Radius**, **Height**, and **Rotation Segments** to **13.78**, **1.5**, and **50**, respectively. On **AM | topGeo | Caps PG**, turn on the **Fillet** switch and then set **Segment** and **Radius** to **5** and **0.15**, respectively.

Create another cylinder for the central part and rename it as **centerGeo**. On **AM | centerGeo | Object PG**, set **Radius**, **Height**, and **Rotation Segments** to **1.3**, **38**, and **18**, respectively. Align the two cylinders [see Figure E2]. Click **Tube** on the **Object** command group to add a tube in the editor view. Rename the tube as **tubeGeo**. On **AM | tubeGeo | Object PG**, set **Inner Radius**, **Outer Radius**, **Rotation Segments**, and **Height** to **1.3**, **4**, **50**, and **2**, respectively. Align the **tubeGeo** at the bottom of the **centerGeo** [see Figure E3].

Now, we are going to create support for the table. Create a cube in the viewport and then rename it as **supportGeo**. On **AM | supportGeo | Object PG**, set **Size X, Size Y, Size Z** to **1.6**, **12.8**, and **2.1**, respectively. Also, check the **Fillet** switch and then set **Fillet Radius** and **Fillet Subdivisions** to **0.1** and **3**, respectively.

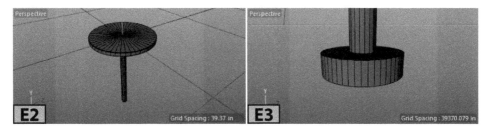

Ensure **supportGeo** is selected in **OM** and then on **SP | Deformer** command group, press and hold LMB on **Bend** . Click **Taper** with the **Shift** held down.

What just happened?
*Here, I have applied the **Taper** modifier to the **supportGeo**. Holding down **Shift** ensures that **Taper** object will be child of the **supportGeo** otherwise it will be added at the same level as the **suppportGeo**. The **Deformer** objects deform the geometry of the other objects. You can use **Deformer** objects with primitive objects, Generator objects, polygon splines and splines. Keep the following in mind while working with deformers:*

- *The Deformer object affects only its parent.*
- *You can apply a number of Deformer objects on an object.*
- *The order of the deformers is also important.*
- *The Deformer objects are evaluated from top to bottom.*
- *The Deformer objects have its origin and orientation.*
- *All deformers are activated automatically when you create them. The Deformer objects have a green check mark next to them in OM. A Deformer object has no effect if it is deactivated.*

On **AM | Taper | Object PG**, click **Fit To Parent**. Set **Strength** to **40** and turn on the **Fillet** switch.

Tip: Taper Strength
You can interactive change the strength in the viewport by dragging the orange line [see Figure E4].

Align the **supportGeo** with **tubeGeo** [see Figure E5].

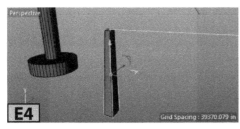

Now, we will work on the roller. Create a cube and then set its **Size X**, **Size Y**, **Size Z** to **0.3**, **0.926**, and **0.6**, respectively. Set **Segment Y** to **15**. Apply a **Bend** modifier to the cube using the **Shift** key. On **AM | Bend | Object PG**, click **Fit to Parent** and then set **Strength** to **180**. Now, align the cube [see Figure E6]. Now, create a cylinder and align it [see Figure E7]. Group the cube and cylinder that you just created with the name **rollerGrp**. Group **rollerGrp** and **supportGeo** with the name **baseGrp**.

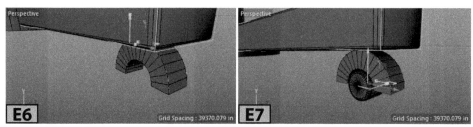

Switch to the Top view and ensure the **baseGrp** is selected. Press **L** to invoke the **Enable Axis** mode and then move the axis at the center of the **topGeo** using the **Move Tool** ⊕ [see Figure E8]. Press **L** again to disable the **Enable Axis** mode. Enable snapping for easily aligning axis.

What just happened?

*Here, I've moved the origin of the group to the center of the model so that when I create copies of the **baseGrp**, they are rotated correctly around the new axis center. You can quickly enable/disable the **Enable Axis** mode using the L key. Keep the following in mind:*

- *When you rotate or move axes of a hierarchical object, all axes of the child objects will also get affected.*
- *Before animating objects ensure that you define the axis because if you rotate the parent, error will occur in the animation tracks of the child. The error occurs because of the change in the axes of the parent object.*
- *You cannot move axis while working with primitive object. You need to make the object editable [first selecting it and then pressing **C**]. The workaround for primitive is that you make it child of a **Null** object and then move axis. The quickest way to enclose an object inside a **Null**, select the object and press **Alt+G**.*
- *Do not make multiple selections in **OM** when you are temporarily make axis changes.*

Now, using the **Array** object 🍡 from the **Modeling Objects** command group to create four more copies of the **baseGrp** [see Figure E9].

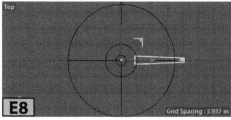

Practical Tests

Test 1: Creating a Road Side Sign

Create a model of a road side sign [see Figure P1].

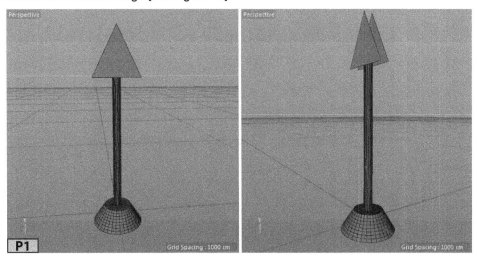

Hint Test – 1

*Create the model using the **Cone**, **Cylinder**, and **Polygon** primitive objects.*

Test 2: Creating a Robo

Create a robot model [see Figure P2].

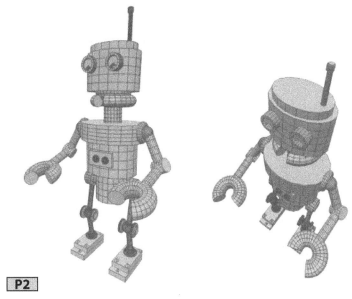

Hint Test – 2

*Create the model using the **Cube**, **Sphere**, **Cylinder**, **Pyramid**, **Cone**, **Torus**, and Tube primitive objects.*

Test 3: Coffee Table
Create the coffee table model [see Figure P3] using the **Cube** primitive.

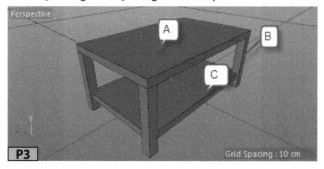

Test 3 Dimensions:
A: *Length=35.433", Width=21.654", Height=1.5"*
B: *Length=34.037", Width=20.8", Height=1.5"*
C: *Length=2", Width=2", Height=13.78"*

Test 4: 8-Drawer Dresser
Create the 8-Drawer Dresser model [see Figure P4] using the **Cube** primitive.

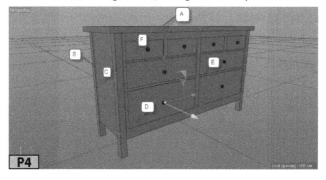

Test 4 Dimensions:
A: *Length=65", Width=21", Height=1.5"*
B: *Length=2", Width=2", Height=35"*
C: *Length=60.76", Width=18.251", Height=30"*
D: *Length=27.225", Width=19.15", Height=11"*
E: *Length=27.225", Width=19.15", Height=7"*
F: *Length=12.871", Width=19.15", Height=5"*

Test 5: Foot Stool

Create the foot stool model [see Figure P5] using the **Cylinder** and **Box** primitives.

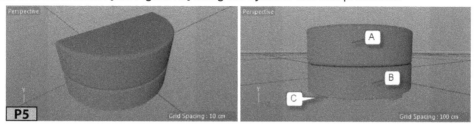

Test 5 Dimensions:

A: Radius=14", Height=5.91", and Fillet=0.32"
B: Radius=14", Height=7.5", and Fillet=0.74"
C: Length=1.651", Width=3.455", Height=1.496", and Fillet=0.087"

Summary

In this unit, the following topics are covered:

- Navigating the workspace
- Customizing the interface
- Understanding various UI components
- Setting preferences for CINEMA 4D
- Understanding layouts
- Moving, rotating, and scaling objects
- Managers, and Browsers
- Getting help

This page intentionally left blank

Unit CI2: Tools of the Trade

In the last unit, you learned how to create and place objects in the scene view. In this unit, I will describe how you can place and arrange these objects accurately using arrange tools, guides, and **Workplanes**. You will learn to add annotations to the objects in the editor view so that you can mark objects in a complex scene for easy identification. Moreover, you will learn to create the virtual walkthrough. CINEMA 4D offers many tools that let you accomplish complex challenges easily. These tools are available in the **Tools** menu of the main menubar. This unit deals with these tools.

In this unit, I will describe the following:

- Creating guides in the editor view
- Interactively placing lights and adjusting their attributes in the scene
- Measuring angles and distances
- Working with **Workplanes**
- Arranging, duplicating, and randomizing objects
- Correcting lens distortions
- Creating virtual walkthroughs

Guide Tool

 The **Guide Tool** allows you to interactively create guidelines in the viewports. You can use handles of these guidelines to snap other entities such as vertices to them. You can create guidelines in one of the following ways:

Click on a viewport to create a handle, click again to create the second handle. Now, press **ESC** to create a guide [see Figure F1]. A red line appears, click-drag the line to create a guide surface perpendicular the view [see Figure F2].

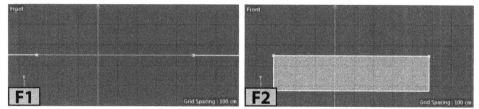

Click on a viewport to create a handle, click again to create the second handle. Don't release the mouse button and drag the mouse pointer and then click to create the guide surface.

To create a segmented guideline, click on a viewport to create a handle, click again to create the second handle. Now, a click within these handles creates a segmented guide [see Figure F3]. To create a duplicate guide, click-drag one of the handles of the guide with **Ctrl** held down [see Figure F4].

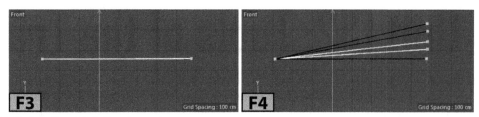

Tip: The Delete Enabled Guides tool

*The **Delete Enabled Guides** tool deletes all guidelines which are active in the **Object Manager**. The active guidelines have green tick mark next to them [see Figure F5]. No prior selection is required to delete the active guidelines.*

Tip: Guides and Snaps

*The guides work in combination with all **Snap** options.*

Video: UCI2-01.mp4

Lighting Tool

This tool allows you to interactively create, select, and place a light object in the viewports. Also, it allows you to adjust the brightness of the lights without using the **Attribute Manager**. Here's the process:

Invoke the **Lighting Tool** from the **Tools** menu. Click on the empty area of the editor view to create a light source. Each click in the empty area of the editor will create a new light. Each new light will inherit the properties of the previously created light. If you click-drag the light, you can move it vertically in the editor view. If one or more lights are selected, these lights will be edited when the surface is manipulated.

If lights already exist in the scene, most relevant light for a surface will automatically be marked when you place the mouse pointer on a surface. While manipulating the light, you can:

- Press **Shift** to move the light source in the direction of the current normals. You can control the distance between the light and surface using **Shift**.
- Press **Ctrl** to adjust the brightness of the light source.
- Press **Ctrl+Shift** to adjust the cone of the spot light.
- Press **Alt** to temporarily switch to the **Target** mode to adjust the target of the spot lights.

Caution: The Lighting Tool

*The functionality of this tool is limited with the generated objects such as **Arrays** and **Cloners** unless you make the objects editable. When deformer objects are used it might be cumbersome to locate the surface. In such cases, hide the **Deformer** object.*

Video: UCI2-02.mp4

Naming Tool

 This tool allows you to efficiently rename object hierarchies in your scene. Although, this tool is specifically built for naming character rigs. However, you can use it to rename tag, material, layer, and Take names. You can also use this tool to save already corrected named hierarchies as a preset and then use the preset to rename other hierarchies.

To understand working of this tool, create a series of five joints in the scene using the **Joint Tool** and then rename them as **Hip**, **Knee**, **Foot**, **Ball**, and **Toe** [see Figure F6]. Now, select **Hip** from the **Attribute Manager** and then choose **Naming Tool** from the **Tools** menu. In the **Attribute Manager**, click **Add** from the **Options** group. The **Name** dialog appears. In this dialog, type name as **leg** and click **OK**. Now, select **leg** from the **Type** drop-down. Enter **L_** in the **Prefix** field and **_$N** in the **Suffix** field. Now, click **Apply Name** to rename the objects [see Figure F7]. The **$N** string is used to number objects automatically.

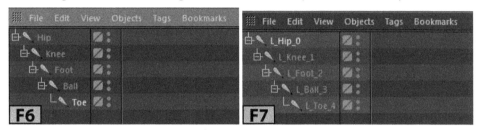

Now, for example, if you want to rename the hierarchy for the right leg, enter **L_** in the **Replace** field and **R_** in the **With** field. Click **Replace Name** to rename the objects [see Figure F8].

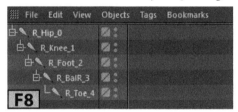

Video: UCI2-03.mp4

Measure & Construction Tool

You can use this tool to measure distance and angle between two objects. The measurement can be stored in a measurement object for later use. You can also adjust the distance and angles numerically after taking the measurement.

To measure distance, choose the **Measure & Construction Tool** from the **Tools** menu and enable snapping. Press and hold **Ctrl+Shift** and drag the mouse pointer from one point to another point to measure distance. To measure a new distance, click **New Measure** in the **Attribute Manager | Measure & Construction | Options** group. Repeat the process to measure the new distance. To measure an angle, **Ctrl** click on the point where the line should end. Now, you can change the distance and angle values from the **Attribute Manager** or directly in the viewport by dragging the values. To move arrowheads, drag them with the **Shift** [red arrowheads] or **Ctrl** [green arrowheads] held down.

Video: UCI2-04.mp4

You can also use this tool to move individual points, edges, and polygons of an object.

See Video: UCl2-05.mp4

Annotation Tool

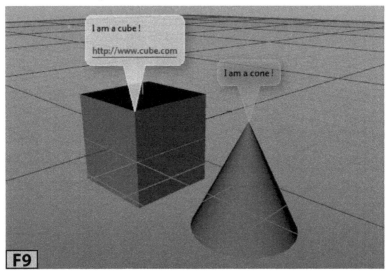 This tool is used to interactively create **Annotation** tags in the viewports [see Figure F9]. These tag are very useful in adding object-specific comments to the objects in a complex scene. The text fields move with the corresponding object. If the object is not visible, the corresponding text fields will also not be visible in the viewport.

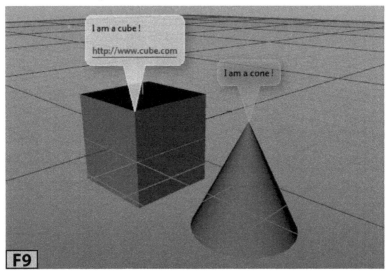

To create a tag, press and hold the LMB on the object, a red cursor appears. This cursor snaps to the valid object points. If you release the mouse button without snapping the cursor, the annotation is snapped to the center point of the object. You can press **ESC** to abort the creation process. When you create an annotation, an **Annotation** tag is applied to the object. Once you create an annotation, you can change the **Annotation** text and URL from the **Attribute Manager**.

You can double-click on a field, to unfold as well as activate it. If you hover the mouse pointer on the annotations, the folded and scaled down boxes will be maximized temporarily. **Ctrl+Shift** clicking on a field toggles the scale of the field.

Note: The WWW tag
*The older **WWW** tag will be automatically converted to the **Annotation** tags when loaded in CINEMA 4D.*

See Video: UCl2-06.mp4

Workplanes

The **Workplanes** are primarily designed for use in the technical modeling in which elements are arranged along perpendicular axis. The **Workplanes** are generally used in the **Perspective** view. You can use the **Workplanes** to place and arrange objects across a plane. However, the position, scale, and rotation will always be according to the world coordinate system. This system always remains visible as a light gray grid in a viewport.

Tip: Default workplane settings
To switch back to default settings [the world grid], choose **Workplanes** | **Align Workplane to Y**  *from the* **Tools** *menu.*

Align Workplane to X, Align Workplane to Y, Align Workplane to Z

 You can use these commands to arrange the *Workplane* to the respective axis. The normals will be always oriented along the Y-axis. The **Align Workplane to Y** mode is the most commonly used command, as it resembles the world grid.

Align Workplane to Selection

 This command rotates the **Workplane** according to the currently selected element.

Align Selection to Workplane

 This command positions the selected elements on the **Workplane**.

See Video: UCI2-07.mp4

Arranging Objects

Cinema 4D offers many tools to arrange objects in the scene. Let's explore them.

Arrange

This command allows you to arrange, scale, or rotate selected objects. When you change the attributes in the **Attribute Manager**, real-time feedback is displayed in the viewports. To arrange objects, select objects and then choose **Arrange Objects** | **Arrange** from the **Tool** menu. In the **Attribute Manager**, set the desired **Mode**, and then click **Apply** if the objects are not instantly arranged in the viewport. Now, adjust the settings in the **Attribute Manager** as long as the **Arrange** function is active.

See Video: UCI2-08.mp4, and UM1-09.mp4

Center

This command allows you to center objects in the 3D space in the viewports. This command is applied to all selected objects in the **Object Manager**. However, the children of the selected objects are not affected. An object in CINEMA 4D is enclosed inside a cuboid of bounding box. The axis system used for alignment considers the center of the axis at the center of the bounding box.

See Video: UCI2-10.mp4

Duplicate

 This command allows you to create as many as duplicates you want to create depending on the RAM available. You can also transform duplicates using this command. Most of the options available for this tool are similar to that of the **Arrange** command.

See Video: UCI2-11.mp4

Transfer

 This function allows you to copy the **PSR** values [position, rotation, and scale] from one object to another. To transfer values, select the object[s] you want to modify and then execute the **Transfer** command. Now, hover the mouse over the source object, a white line appears. Click to transfer values.

See Video: UCI2-12.mp4

Randomize

You can use this function to randomly place objects in 3D space. You can also randomize the scale and rotation of the objects. To randomize objects, select them and then execute the **Randomize** command.

See Video: UCI2-13.mp4

Lens Distortion

The **Lens Distortion** tool allows you to deal with the lens distortion effects in CINEMA 4D. You can correct the distortion in the image shot with the small focal lengths [shot with wide angles]. This distortion can be problematic while motion tracking a footage. The motion tracking produces better results when used with the distortion free footage. The distortions can be classified as barrel distortion, pincushion distortion, and mustache distortions. Figure 10 shows the barrel, pincushion, and mustache distortion, respectively. The live footage generally have the barrel shaped distortions. You can use the **Lens Distortion** tool to create a lens profile that you can use later when tracking a live footage.

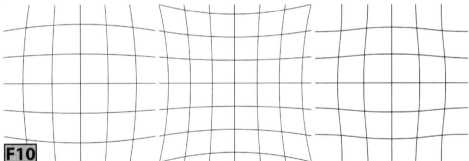
F10

There are two algorithms that you can use to solve the distortion: **Manual** and **Automatic**. The **Manual** method is for the experienced users in which the tool's settings are manually adjusted. The **Automatic** method is the recommended method and works well in most of the situations.

You can use the **Lens Distortion** tool to create guides in the image. Try to match the guides with the curved lines [the lines that should be straight] on the image. You can **Ctrl+Drag** a guide to create duplicates. **Ctrl+Click** once on a guide to create a new point on the line. You can delete the selected point by using **Backspace** or **Del**.

See Video: UCI2-14.mp4

Keep the following in mind while creating lens profiles:

- Place guides precisely. The more guides [precise] you use, the better result you get.
- The lens distortion is calculated accurately where the density of guide is more, however, the rears with low number of guides can be calculated incorrectly. Therefore, you need to place and spread out guides strategically.
- To restore the size of the original image after correction, you can modify the scale of the image as well as its offset values.

Doodle

The options available for **Doodle** allow you to sketch in the editor view. You can use this tool to mark corrections, make notes, load bitmaps, and so forth. These options work well with a tablet, however, you can use a mouse as well. When draw in the editor view, each drawing is saved in a doodle object in a frame.

Tip: Rendering Doodle
By default, the Render Doodle option is active in Render Settings | Options. As a result, the doodles appear in the render output and this is the reason you can only draw doodle in the Render Safe area of the viewport.

See Video: UCI2-15.mp4

Virtual Walkthrough

There are two tools available allow you to walk or fly through your CINEMA 4D scenes. This experience is similar to a third-person shooter game where you can walk or fly though the scene. You can record a camera path can be recorded or can be output as spline. A virtual walkthrough can be created in CINEMA 4D using one of the following methods:

- Use the **Virtual Walkthrough** tool to fly freely through the scene. To exit this mode, select any other tool.
- Use the **Collision Orbit** tool to define an orbital path around an object.
- Use the **Collision Detection** tag to exclude specific objects such as doors from the collision detection.

Keep in mind the following while working with these tools:

- If you stuck somewhere in the scene [due to collision detection] and not able to move, press **Ctrl** to temporarily deactivate the detection.
- These tools works with the polygonal objects. If you face any issue with the geometry, make it editable by selecting it first and then pressing **C**.
- These tools behave correctly if a floor [polygonal object] is used in the scene.

Collision Orbit Tool

 You can use this tool in conjunction with the **Target Camera** to orbit around an object. The camera will automatically avoid the obstacles. To understand working of this tool:

- Create a **Target Camera** in the scene.
- Target the object [around which you want to orbit] using the **Camera's Null**.
- Switch to the target camera.

- Invoke the **Collision Orbit** tool and move the mouse in the 3D view with LMB held down. The **HP** rotation values will be displayed in the **HUD** in the viewport. The motion path can be recorded.

The collision is detected when the camera's z-axis [path of the view] intersects with the given object. A green icon appears when this happens.

See Video: UCI2-16.mp4

Virtual Walkthrough Tool

 You can use this tool to fly around the scene. The mouse and keyboard can be used to navigate the scene as you do in a 3D third person shooter game.

See Video: UCI2-17.mp4

3D Connexion

The option available for **3D Connexion** work with the 3D mouse sometimes also referred to as **Spacemouse**. This mouse offers six directions for movement. CINEMA 4D uses the 3DxWare driver to operate the Spacemouse. It is must that you install the driver before starting the 3D mouse.

Practical Test
Test 1: Arranging Objects
Create a text [Love] using **Cube** primitive, **Arrange** and **Duplicate** functions [see Figure P1].

Hint Test – 1
*Create a spline using the **Sketch** tool along which the cubes will be duplicated. Create another spline using the **Pen** tool that will be used to rotate the cubes, see Figure P2. Use the **Duplicate** function to create **100** copies of the cube and then use the **Arrange** function to arrange duplicate cubes on the spline.*

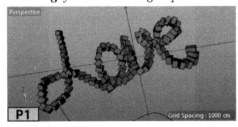 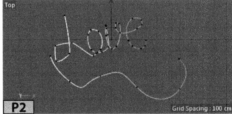

Summary
This unit covered the following topics:

- Creating guides in the editor view
- Interactively placing lights and adjusting their attributes in the scene
- Measuring angles and distances
- Working with Workplanes
- Arranging, duplicating, and randomizing objects
- Correcting lens distortions
- Creating virtual walkthroughs

Unit CM1: Spline Modeling

Splines are a sequences of vertices, connected by lines [segments] lying in 3D space. However, a spline has no 3-dimnesional depth. The splines are infinitely thin entities and are not visible during the rendering. However, if you are using Studio version of CINEMA 4D, you can render splines using Hair, and Sketch & Toon features. The shape of these lines is defined by the interpolation method. The interpolation method defines whether shape of the line is curved or straight. The curved splines have a soft leading edge without any sharp corner. In this unit, I will cover the spline modeling tools and techniques.

In this unit, I will describe the following:

- Splines tools and modeling techniques
- Generator command group

A spline is made up of several partial curves called lines or segments. You can create holes using splines, when a spline lies completely inside another splines and both splines are closed. If two segments overlap, no 3D surface will be created or you will see strange results.

CINEMA 4D offers a number of predefines parametric splines curves known as Spline primitives. These primitives are calculated using the mathematical formulas and therefore they have no points [vertices] to edit. You can convert a parametric spline primitive to an editable spline by first selecting it and then pressing **C**. To adjust vertices using the **Pen** tool [I will discuss is shortly], you must make the spline editable. However, you can apply **Deformers** to a spline even if the spline has not been made editable. You can access spline primitives from the **Spline** option of the **Create** menu or from the **Spine** command group from the **Standard** palette [see Figure F1].

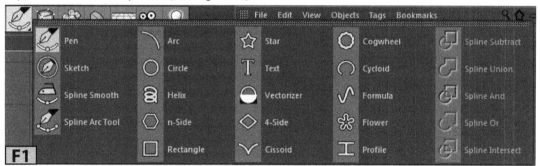

Working with Spline Tools

CINEMA 4D offers four tools for drawing splines: **Spline Pen**, **Sketch**, **Spline Smooth**, and **Spline Arch Tool**.

Spline Sketch Tool

In R17 version of CINEMA 4D, the old **Freehand** tool is replaced by the **Spline Sketch Tool** and it can do lot more than the old tool. This tool works well with tablets. You can use this tool to directly draw in the viewport and to edit the exiting splines. For example, you can use it to redirect, smooth, and connect splines. This tool obeys the snap settings. The snap settings are particularly useful when you want to draw a curve on the surface of an object.

To draw spline using this tool, invoke it, and then click and drag in the editor view. As soon as you release the LMB the spline will be created.

Here're some functions of this tool:

- You can grab a spline from any location and edit it from that location.
- You can connect two splines [connected at their ends] or two segments of the same spline. If you connect start and end points of a spline, the spline will be closed. You can also connect two splines or two segments of the same spline anywhere along the spline.
- You can temporarily switch to the **Spline Smooth Tool** by pressing the **Shift** key. The previous defined settings of the **Spline Smooth Tool** will be used.
- If you want to unify spline segments or two separate splines, select the splines first. MMB drag to specify the radius of the brush interactively, and then drag in the view to connect the splines. Two separate splines will be combined into one. *Video: UCM1-01.mp4.*

Spline Smooth Tool

This tool not only allows you to smooth the splines but also offers a number of other features [works as a shaping brush] that can be combined seamlessly. You can adjust the strength and radius of this tool interactively by dragging the mouse pointer vertically or horizontally. This tool can create lot of points on the spline when you are using feature such as random. You can fix this by switching to the **Smooth** mode.

See Video: UCM1-02.mp4.

Spline Arch Tool

 You can use this tool to create variety of arc shapes and soft connection between segments. This tool creates 3 point circle and obeys snap settings. To create an arch three points are required: start point, middle point, and end point.

See Video: UCM1-03.mp4.

Pen Tool

 This tool is used to create or edit splines. It replaces the previous **Bézier**, **B-Spline**, **Linear** and **Akima Spline** tools and provides a wide variety of new functions. To create a spline, invoke the tool and then click on the view to create a point. If you drag the mouse pointer, a tangent is created to produce a curved section. A ghost preview of the next segment is shown before you create the next point. It helps in visualizing the next segment that will created if click to create next point.

Here're some functions of this tool:

- This tool obeys the snapping settings.
- The points created using this tool can be selected and moved without need of selecting them.

- If you click on a segment using this tool, the neighboring points will be selected.
- You can make multiple selections using **Shift**.
- When you click on a point or segment, the tangents are displayed and can be edited.
- If you want to extend a spline at the beginning or at the end, select the respective point and then click to create a new point. If a point is selected along the spline [other than the end point], press **Ctrl** to continue at the spline's end.
- If you position the mouse pointer on a segment, it will be highlighted. RMB click shows a menu with number of options that you can use to edit splines.
- Splines points and segments can be moved by clicking and dragging on them. If you press **Shift** and then drag the tangent handles, the tangents will be broken and the selection will be manipulated between the neighboring points.
- Double-clicking on a broken tangent straightens it and set both halves to same length.
- Double-clicking on a point toggles between the soft tangent [both halves have same length] and null tangent.
- If you hover mouse over the spline with **Ctrl** held down, a preview appears that shows where a matching tangent will be inserted.
- If you connect the start and end points of a spline, the spline will be closed.
- You can also connect sections of a single spline. If the spline contains other open sections, a new spline will be created.

As mentioned above, if you RMB click on a point or segment, a popup menu appears with several options. The following table summarizes these options.

Table 1: The context popup menu options

Option	Description
Delete Point	Deletes the selected point. You can also delete a point by **Ctrl** clicking on it.
Disconnect Point	Disconnects the spline at the selected point. If spline is a closed spline, the spline will be separated at the selected location and both end points will have the same shared location.
Hard Tangents	Creates an angular point by setting tangent length of the **Bezier** splines to **0**.
Soft Tangents	Sets equal length for the both halves of the tangent and creates a soft curve.
Kill Edge	Deletes the spline section.
Add Point	Adds a new point at the clicked location.
Split Point	Adds two new, non-coherent, congruent points at the clicked location of the segment. The spline will be split into sections.
Hard Edge	The tangents length will be set to zero thus the spline will be made linear. Double-clicking on a point do the same.
Soft Edge	The spline will be made curve. Double-clicking on a point do the same.

Note: Spline Tools, Commands, and Options
*The tools, commands, and options available in CINEMA 4D for changing the shape of the splines can be accessed from the **Mesh** menu and are discussed in next unit.*

Working with Generators

The tools available in the Generator command group are some of the most powerful tools of [**Extrude, Subdivision Surface**] CINEMA 4D that allows you to create surfaces quickly, see Figure F2. You can also access these tools from the **Generators** sub-menu of the **Create** menu. The **Generators** are interactive, they use other objects to generate their surfaces. The following table summarizes the Generators.

Table 2: The Generators

Option	Icon	Description
Subdivision Surface		This tool is one of the most powerful sculpting tool offered by CIENMA 4D to a digital artist. You can create almost any shape using the point weighting, and edge weighting. This tool uses an algorithm to subdivide and round the object. You can use any kind of object with this tool, however, most of the times, you will work with polygons. You need to make the object child of the **Subdivision Surface** object.
Extrude		You can use this tool to extrude a spline to create an object with depth.
Lathe		When you apply this tool on a spline, it rotates the spline about the Y axis of the local axis system of the **Generator** object to generate a surface of revolution.
Loft		Use this tool to stretch a skin over two or more splines.
Sweep		This tool works with two or three splines. The first spline referred to as contour spline, defines the cross section and is swept along the second spline, referred to as path. The optional third spline, referred to as rail spline, controls the scale of the contour spline over the object's length.
Bezier		This tool stretches a surface over Bezier curves in the X and Y directions.

Hands-on Exercises

Before you start the hands-on exercises, let's first create a project folder that will host the exercise files. Open the **Windows Explorer** and navigate to the folder **c4dr17studio** in the **C** drive of your system. Create a sub-folder with the name **unit-cm1** in the **c4dr17studio** folder.

Exercise 1: Creating a Pear

In this exercise, you will model a pear using splines and **Lathe** generator [see Figure E1].

 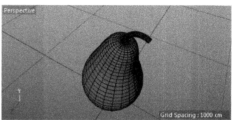

The following table summarizes the exercise:

Table E1: Creating a Pear	
Skill level	Beginner
Time to complete	20 Minutes
Topics in the section	• Getting Started • Creating the Pear Model
Project Folder	c4dr17studio/unit-cm1
Units	Centimeters
Final exercise file	ucm1-hoe1-end.c4d

Getting Started

Ensure that you have access to the **pear.jpg** in the **\cinema4dr17studio\unit-m1** folder. Start a new scene in CINEMA 4D and set units to **Centimeters**.

Creating the Pear Model

Open **Windows Explorer** and drag the **pear.jpg** to the **Front** view. Press **Shift+V** to open the **Viewport [Front]** options in **AM**. In **AM | Back PG**, set **Transparency** to **65%** and **Offset Y** to **435** so that bottom of the pear sits on the origin [see Figure E2]. Choose **Pen** ✏ from **SP | Spline** command group and then click and drag to the origin to create the first point. Follow the pear shape to create a profile curve [see Figure E3] and then press **ESC** to complete the creation of the curve. Don't worry about the exact placement of the curve. You can always come back and adjust the points using the **Pen** tool.

Select the bottom point and then enter **0** in the **Position [X]** and **Position [Y]** fields in **CM** to place the point at the origin point. Similarly, select the top point and set its **Position [X]** to **0**. Ensure spline is selected and then click **SP | Generator** command group | **Lathe** 🍶 with **Alt** held down to connect **Lathe** object to the **Spline**. Switch to the **Perspective** view to see the shape of the pear. Press **NB** to enable the **Gouraud Shading (Lines)** mode [see Figure E4].

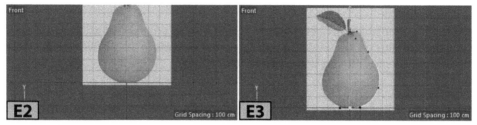

Select **Spline** in **OM** and then in **AM | Object PG**, choose **Natural** from the **Intermediate Points** drop-down. Now, set **Numbers** to **10** [see Figure E5].

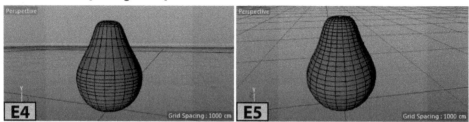

The options in the **Intermediate Points** drop-down define how the spline is further subdivided with the intermediate points. This setting only affects when spline is used with the generator objects. When you select the **Natural** method for interpolation, the **Number** field corresponds to the number of intermediate points between vertices. The points on the curvature are positioned closer together where is the spline has more curvature.

Ensure **Lathe** is selected in **OM** and then click **Bend** from **SP | Deformer** command group, to add a **Bend** object. Ensure the order of the objects, as shown in Figure E6. On **AM | Bend | Object PG**, click **Fit to Parent**. Set **Size [Y]** to **430** and **Strength** to **-16** [see Figure E7].

Now, you will create a stem for the pear. Create a **Cylinder** primitive. On **AM | Cylinder | Object PG**, set **Radius**, **Height**, **Height Segments**, and **Rotation Segments** to **6**, **79**, **24**, and **24**, respectively. Align it to the top of the cylinder [see Figure E8]. Apply a **Bend** modifier to it and then on **AM | Bend | Object PG**, click **Fit to Parent**. Set **Strength** to **-120** to bend the stem [see Figure E9].

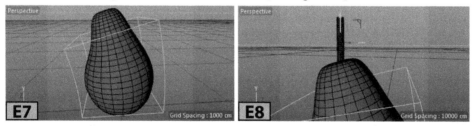

Note: Subdivisions
*If you want to increase the number of subdivisions along the rotation of the curve, select the spline and then on AM | Lathe | Object PG, change the value of the **Subdivision** field. You can use the **Isoparm Subdivision** to define the*

*number of isoparms used to display the **Lathe** object when the isoparms display mode is active. Press **NI** to activate this mode. Figure E10 shows the pear mode with **Isoparm Subdivision** set to **12**.*

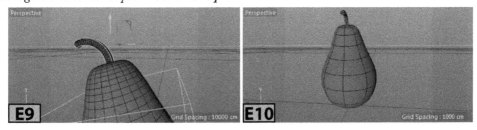

Exercise 2: Creating a Glass Bottle and Liquid

In this exercise, you will model a glass bottle and liquid using the **Lathe** generator [see Figure E1].

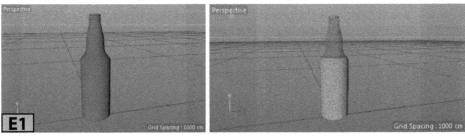

The following table summarizes the exercise:

Table E2: Creating a Glass Bottle and Liquid	
Skill level	Intermediate
Time to complete	35 Minutes
Topics in the section	• Getting Started • Creating the Bottle • Creating the Liquid
Project Folder	c4dr17studio/unit-cm1
Units	Centimeters
Final exercise file	ucm1-hoe2-end.c4d

Getting Started

Ensure that you have access to the **beer.jpg** in the **\cinema4dr17studio\unit-m3** folder. Start a new scene in CINEMA 4D and set units to **Centimeters**.

Creating the Bottle

Open **Windows Explorer** and drag the **beer.jpeg** to the **Front** view. Press **Shift+V** to open the **Viewport [Front]** options in AM. In **AM | Back PG**, set **Size X** and **Size Y** to **400**. Also, set **Transparency** to **65%** and **Offset Y** to **188** so that bottom of the bottle sits on the origin. Create a shape using the **Spline Pen** tool [see Figure E2]. Rename the spline as **bottle**. Select the bottom point and set its **X** and **Y** positions to **0**.

Press **Spacebar** to activate **Live Selection** tool and then RMB click on bottle in editor view. Choose **Create Outline** from the menu and then drag the spline to create an outline [see Figure E3]. Notice that the **Create Outline** function created a closed spline. On **AM | bottle | Object PM**, turn off the **Close Spline** switch. Select the second point from the bottom and make sure its **X** position is set to **0** [see Figure E4].

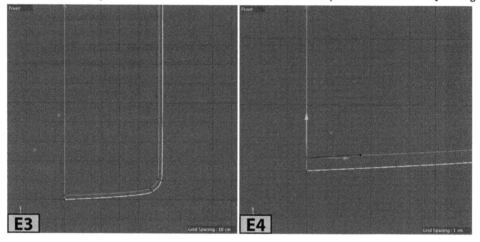

Select the points at the top [see Figure E5] and then press **Delete** to make a straight inside of the bottle. Now, apply a **Lathe** generator to create shape of the bottle [see Figure E6].

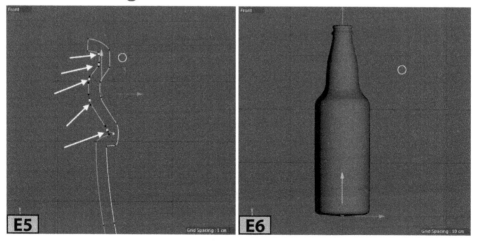

Creating the Liquid

Now, you will create the liquid geometry. Turn off the **Lathe** object ⬭ . Select inside points of the bottle [see Figure E7]. RMB click on bottle in editor view and then choose **Split** from the menu to create a new spline. On **OM**, drag the new spline out of the **Lathe** group and rename it as liquid. Select the top two points of the liquid [see Figure E8] and then press **Delete** to remove the points.

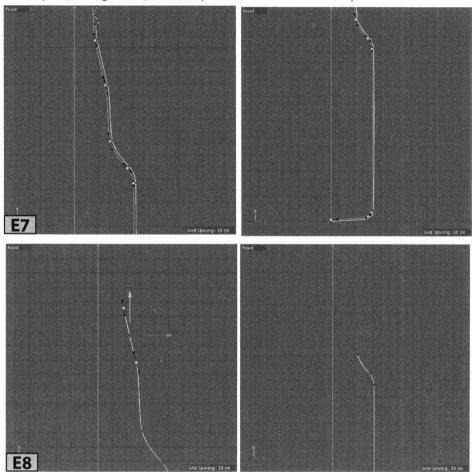

Tip: Liquid Level

*If you want to create a different height for the liquid, RMB click on the spline and then choose **Knife** from the menu. You can also press **MK**. Now, create a cut on the spline on the desired height and delete the points. The **Knife** tool lets you to cut polygon and spline objects. The tool works in all three modes: **point**, **edge** and **polygon**.*

Using the **Pen** tool ✍, drag the top point of the liquid to the vertical green line [see Figure E9]. RMB click on the point and then choose **Hard Tangents** from the menu. Align the top points of the liquid to get an even surface. Now, create the liquid geometry by applying a **Lathe** generator ⬭ object to the **liquid** spline.

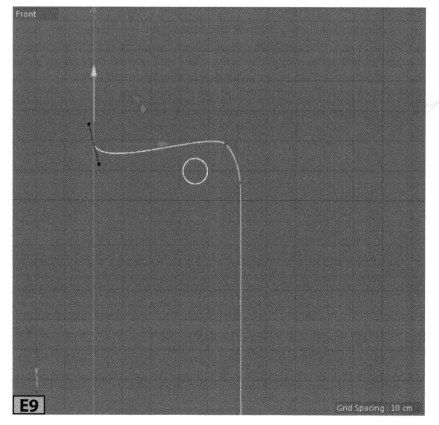

Exercise 3: Creating a Martini Glass

In this exercise, you will model a martini glass using **Lathe** generator [see Figure E1].

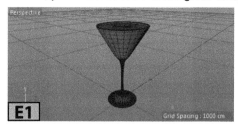 

The following table summarizes the exercise:

Table E3: Creating a Martini Glass	
Skill level	Intermediate
Time to complete	45 Minutes
Topics in the section	• Getting Started • Creating the Glass and Liquid • Creating the Umbrella

Project Folder	c4dr17studio/unit-cm1
Units	Centimeters
Final exercise file	ucm1-hoe3-end.c4d

Getting Started

Ensure that you have access to the **matini-glass.jpg** in the **\cinema4dr17studio\unitm-1** folder. Start a new scene in CINEMA 4D and set units to **Centimeters**.

Creating the Glass and Liquid

Open **Windows Explorer** and drag the **martini-glass.jpg** to the **Front** view. Press **Shift+V** to open the **Viewport [Front]** options in the **AM**. In **AM | Back PG**, set **Size X** and **Size Y** to **300** and **456.472**, respectively. Also, set **Transparency** to **65%** and **Offset Y** to **194** so that bottom of the bottle sits on the origin. Also, set **Offset X** to **2**. Create a shape using the **Spline Pen** tool [see Figure E2]. Now, create the geometry for the glass and liquid, as described in Exercise-2 [see Figure E3].

Creating the Umbrella

Create a cone object in the scene. On **AM | Cone | Object PG**, set **Top Radius**, **Bottom Radius**, and **Height** to **10**, **100**, and **57**, respectively. On the **Cap PG**, turn off the **Caps** switch. Create a cube and then on **AM | Cube | Object PG**, set **Size X**, **Size Y**, and **Size Z** to **120**, **8**, and **8**, respectively. Align it with the cone [see Figure E4].

Select cube in **OM** and press **Alt+G** to group it inside a **Null** object. Press **L** and then move the axis to the center of the cone [see Figure E5]. Press **L** again to disable **Enable Axis** mode. Ensure **Null** is selected in **OM** and then click **Array** on **SP** with **Alt** held down. On **AM | Array | Object PG**, set **Radius** to **0** and **Copies** to **8**. Select **Null** on **OM** and then press the **R** key to activate the **Rotate** tool. Now, rotate the objects along Z-axis [see Figure E6]. You can now modify the dimensions of the cube and cone so that they better fit with each other. Create another cube to make the umbrella stick and align it with the top part of the umbrella.

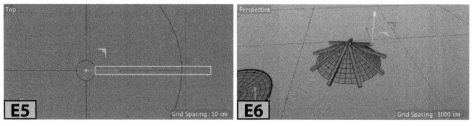

Practical Tests

Test 1: Creating a Bowl

Create a model of bowl using the **Lathe** generator [see Figure P1]. Use **bowl.jpg** as reference.

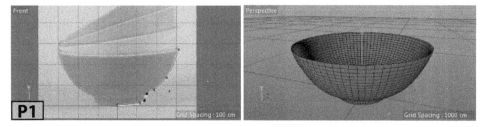

Test 2: Creating a Candle Stand

Create the candle stand model [see Figure P2] using the **Lathe** generator.

Test 3: Creating a Glass Table

Create model of a glass table using the **Rectangle** spline, **Cylinder** primitive, and **Extrude** generator [see Figure P3].

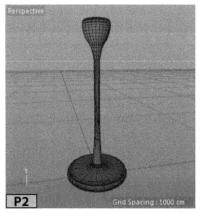

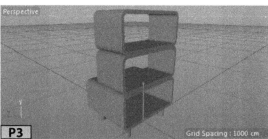

Create model of a corkscrew using the **Helix** spline and **Sweep** generator object [see Figure P4].

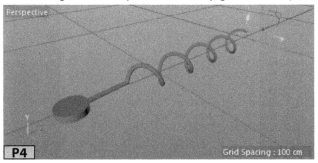

Summary

This unit covered the following topics:

- Splines tools and modeling techniques
- Generator command group

This page intentionally left blank

Unit CM2: Polygon Modeling

Polygons are a type of geometry that you can use to create 3D models in CINEMA 4D. Polygons represent and approximate surfaces of a 3D model. Many 3D modelers use the primitive objects [discussed in Chapter 1] as the basic starting point for creating models and then create complex geometries using the sub-object levels [components] such as points, edges, and polygons. You can also apply commands such as **Bevel**, **Extrude**, **Bridge**, and so forth on a primitive's polygon mesh in order to modify the primitive's shape.

In this unit, I will describe the following:

- Polygons components
- Polygon modeling techniques
- Selection tools
- Polygons structure tools
- Splines structure tools
- Modeling Objects
- Deformers

Closed shapes in a plane with three or more sides are called polygons. The endpoints of the sides of polygons are called points or vertices. The line connecting two points is called an edge. Polygons are classified by how many sides or angles they have. Following list shows types of polygons based on number of sides they have:

- A triangle is a three sided polygon.
- A quadrilateral is a four sided polygon.
- A pentagon is a five sided polygon.
- A hexagon is a six sided polygon.
- A septagon or heptagon is a seven sided polygon.
- An octagon is an eight sided polygon.
- A nonagon is a nine sided polygon.
- A decagon is a ten sided polygon.

There are a variety of techniques that you can use to create 3D polygonal models in CINEMA 4D but before we start creating models, let's first understand the tools, commands, modes and options that are required to build a 3D model. Let's first start with different modes used in polygonal modeling in CINEMA 4D.

Working with Modes

CINEMA 4D provides three modes for polygonal modeling. These modes are: **Points**, **Edges**, and **Polygons**. Before you use these modes, you need to make a primitive object editable. To do this, ensure that the object is selected and then press **C**.

Points

Use the **Points** mode when you want to edit points of an object. When this mode is active, the points appear as small squares. The selected points appear in color. To select points, you can use the selection tools. You can also select them by clicking on points one by one. To add points to the selection, click on them with **Shift** held down. To remove points from selection, **Ctrl+click** on them. To select all points, choose **Select All** from the **Edit** menu. To de-select all points, choose **Deselect All** from the **Edit** menu. To delete selected points, choose **Delete** from the **Edit** menu. Alternatively, you can press **Backspace** or **Delete** key.

Edges

Use this mode to edit the edges of the polygons, selected edges are highlighted in color. You can select edges much the same way as you select points.

Polygons

In CINEMA 4D, you can work on three types of polygons: triangles, quadrangles, and n-gons. You can select polygons much the same way as you select points or edges.

Note: Using Transformation tools
*You can use the **Move**, **Scale** and **Rotate** tools to edit the selected edges, points, or polygons.*

Selecting Objects and Components

In order to make models in any 3D application, you should be able to select objects or sub-objects/ components [points, edges, and polygons]. CINEMA 4D offers various tools and commands for making selections. Let's explore these tools and commands available in the **Select** menu. These options are also available in the **U** hidden menu.

The following table summarizes the tools and options:

Table 1: The selection tools and options			
Tool	**Icon**	**Shortcut**	**Description**
Loop Selection		U~L	Loops are elements that are connected in a shape of a loop. The **Loop Selection** tool allows you to quickly select the loops. Figure F1 shows the loop selection in **Polygons, Edges,** and **Points** mode. If a point is already selected, in one of the modes, press **Ctrl+Shift** and then click on the next element to create a selection between it and the already selected element.
Ring Selection		U~B	The function of this tool is similar to that of the **Loop Selection** tool, however, it select the elements that form a broad ring-shape.
Outline Selection		U~Q	In the **Polygons** mode, it select the edges that outline the selected polygons. To select outline edges, move the mouse pointer over the polygon selection. When the edges that outline polygons change color, click to select edges, see Figure F2. Also, the **Edges** mode gets activated. This tool also works in the **Edges** mode.

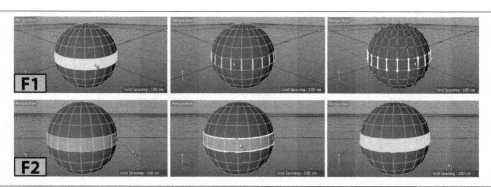

Fill Selection		U~F	In the **Edges** mode, this tool creates a polygon selection from an existing edge selection, see Figure F3.

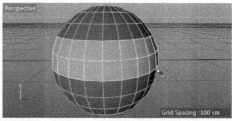

Path Selection		U~M	This tool lets you select polygon edges or points by painting on the edges or points. This tool works only in the **Edges** or **Points** mode, see Figure F4.

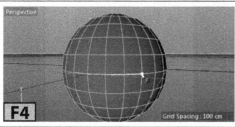
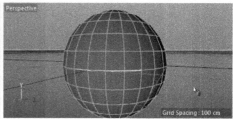

Phong Break Selection	⬭	U~N	This tool works with the low-res mechanical models whose edges are assigned via **Phong Break Shading**.
Select All	⠿		Use this command to select all points, edges, or polygons of the currently selected object.
Deselect All	○○○		Use this command to de-select all points, edges, or polygons of the currently selected object.
Invert	⧄	U~I	Use this command to invert the current selection.

Select Connected	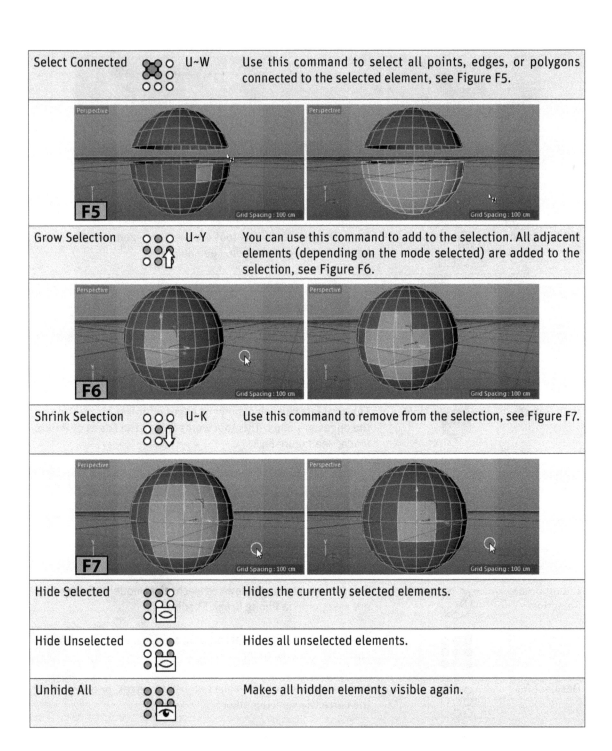 U~W	Use this command to select all points, edges, or polygons connected to the selected element, see Figure F5.

F5

Grow Selection	U~Y	You can use this command to add to the selection. All adjacent elements (depending on the mode selected) are added to the selection, see Figure F6.

F6

Shrink Selection	U~K	Use this command to remove from the selection, see Figure F7.

F7

Hide Selected	Hides the currently selected elements.
Hide Unselected	Hides all unselected elements.
Unhide All	Makes all hidden elements visible again.

Convert Selection U~X		With this command, you can convert one type of selection to another. On executing this command, the **Convert Selection** dialog appears. Select the desired options from the dialog and then click **Convert** to convert the selection, see Figure F8.

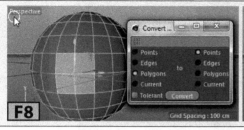 

Invert Visibility		Use this command to make visible elements hidden and hidden elements visible.
Set Vertex Weight		Use this tool to set the vertex weight. To create a vertex map, select the points or polygons and then execute this command, the **Set Vertex Weight** dialog appears. In this dialog, set the value and then click **OK**, see Figure F9.

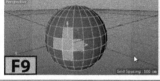  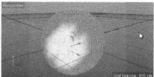

Set Selection		You can use the **Set Selection** command to store selection sets and then recall them later. You can create selection sets for point, edge, and polygon selections. Make a selection and then execute this command, a tag is added to the **Object Manager**. You can manipulate the selection from the **Attribute Manager**, see Figure F10.

Adjusting Structure of the Polygonal Objects

The tools available in the **Mesh** menu are used to change the structures of the polygonal objects. Most of these tools are available in the **Points**, **Edges**, and **Polygons** modes. These tools work on the editable objects. You can make an object editable by choosing **Conversion | Make Editable** from the **Mesh** menu or by pressing **C**. Generally, these tools affect the selected points, edges, or polygons. However, if no component is selected, these tools affect the entire selected objects.

Note: Interactive tools

*Any structure tool that cannot be used on the current selection will be grayed out. For example, if you make a point selection, the **Edge Cut** tool will be grayed out. If you are using an interactive tool, the most recently action can be undone by pressing **Esc** as long as the mouse button is still pressed.*

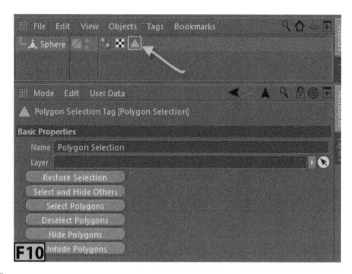

Tip: Using hotkeys

When you are modeling, you can temporarily activate a function using hotkeys. For example, if you select polygons using the **Live Selection** tool, press and hold **D** to temporarily activate the **Extrude** tool. Extrude the polygons and then release the hotkey to switch back to the **Live Selection** tool.

Tip: Modeling popup menu

You can also quickly access the structure tools from the RMB popup menu. The options available in this menu depend on the type of component selected. You can also quickly access these tools from the **U**, and **M** hidden menus.

Tools Parameters

Several tools have their own specific parameters that you can access from the **Options** parameter group of the **Attribute Manager**, see Figure F11. The options in the **Tool** parameter group of the **Attribute Manager** allows you to choose whether the changes will be applied automatically in real-time. If you are working on a heavy scene and your system is responding slowly to the automatic updates, you can disable this feature by turning off the **Realtime Update** switch from the **Attribute Manager | Tool** parameter group, see Figure F12.

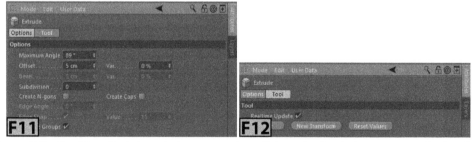

If you turn off the **Realtime Update** switch, you need to click on the **Apply** button to apply the changes to the object. If you want to reapply the tool, click **New Transform**. You can also use this button to repeatedly apply change to the object. For example, if you are using the **Extrude** tool, clicking repeatedly on this button will extrude multiple times. The **Reset** button can be used to reset the tool to its default values.

Following table summarizes the tools, commands, and options available in the **Mesh** menu. This table also summarizes the command, tools, and options that you can apply on the splines.

Table 2: The tools and commands available in the **Mesh** menu

Tool	Icon	Shortcut	Description
Conversion sub-menu			
Make Editable		C	The primitives objects in CINEMA 4D are parametric and created using math formulae. These primitive objects have no points, edges, or polygons. To create complex objects using these primitives, you need to first make the primitive objects editable. When you make an object editable, you get access to the object's components: points, edges, and polygons. You can use the **Make Editable** command to make an object editable. Note that this command is one-way. You cannot convert an editable object back to a parametric object.
Current State to Object			This command allows you to collapse the stack for the selected object and creates a polygon copy of the selected object. For example, if you have applied multiple deformers on an object, you can use this command to create a polygon copy of the resulting shape. If you apply this command to a parametric object, it will create a polygon copy considering all deformers. *Caution: Child Objects* *This command ignores child objects, therefore, you need to apply this command separately for each child object.* *Caution: Animation Data* *The animation data is not copied to the new object when you use this command.*
Connect Objects			You can use this command to create a single object from multiple objects. When you connect the polygonal objects to which you have applied materials and selection tags, CINEMA 4D ensures that selection tags are connected properly. Also, texture projections are restored accurately. *Caution: Animation Data* *The animation data is not copied to the new object when you use this command. The original objects and their animation data is preserved.* If you are connecting splines of different types, the new resulting spline will be a **Bezier** spline.
Connect objects+ Delete			The function of this command is similar to that of the **Connect Objects** command but additionally, it deletes the original objects.

Polygon Groups to Objects		You can use this command to create separate polygonal objects from the from the non-connected surfaces [polygons groups], see Figure F13.

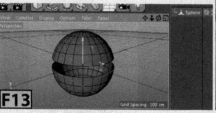 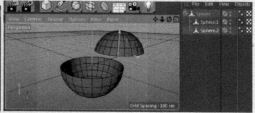

Commands sub-menu

Array		This command allows you to duplicate selected elements [points or polygons] of an object and then distribute them randomly in the 3D world, see Figure F14. You can also vary size as well as rotation of the duplicates. If no elements are selected, all points and surfaces of the selected object are duplicated. You can use this command, for example, to create a complete meadow from a single blade of polygon grass.

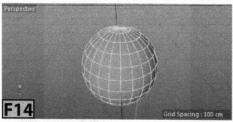 

Clone		Use this command to create duplicate of the surface or points of an object. You can then rotate the duplicated objects along the object axis. The duplicate shown in Figure F15 are created from a cube. The settings use to create the duplicate are shown in the right image of Figure F15.

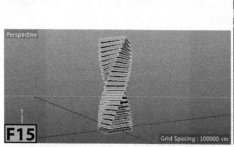 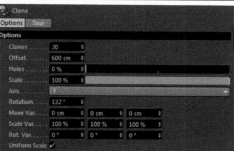

Disconnect		U~D, Shift+D	This command is used to disconnect the selected polygons from the object or segments between the selected spline points, see Figure F16. This command can be applied on splines. Unlike the **Break Segment** tool, the start and end points of the disconnected segments are duplicated and are not deleted from the original spline.

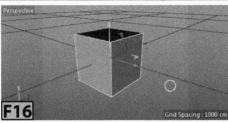 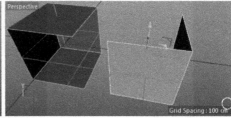

Split		U~P	This command is little bit different than the **Disconnect** command. When you apply this command, the disconnected surfaces create a separate object leaving the original object unchanged.
Collapse		U~C	This command collapses the selected points, edges, or polygons to a single center point. These points can be welded together, see Figure F17.

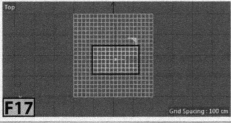 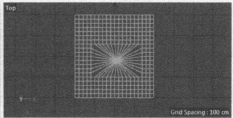

Connect Points/Edges		Alt+X	This command works in the **Points** and **Edges** modes and connects points and edges, see Figures F18 and F19.

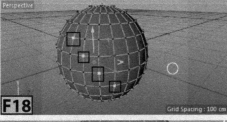 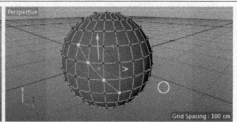

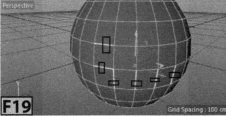 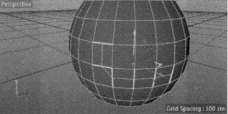

Melt		U~Z	As name suggests, this function melts the selected points, edges, or polygons. Figure F20 shows the melted point, edges, and polygons, respectively.

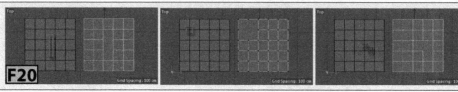

Dissolve			This command works similar to the **Melt** command, however, it deletes the unnecessary points as well. This command is ideal for deleting the unnecessary edges created by the **Connect Points/Edges** command. When you delete the points the phong angle is also taken into account.

However, if you execute this command with **Shift** held down, it deletes all unnecessary points regardless of the Phong angle. In the **Points** and **Polygons** modes, this command exactly works like the **Melt** command. |
| Subdivide | | U~S, Shift+S | This command is used to subdivide polygon objects or splines, see Figure F21. If no elements are selected, it subdivides the whole object.

To define the subdivision level, click on the gear icon next to this command, the **Subdivide** dialog appears. In this dialog, enter the level in the **Subdivision** spinner and then click **OK**. |
| Triangulate | | | This command converts the polygons into triangles, see Figure F22. You might need this command if you are exporting mesh to an application that takes only triangulated geometry.

Note: Triangles
Generally, try to use quads as much as possible during the modeling process. Quads take less memory, they render faster, and produce better shading when used with the subdivision surface. |

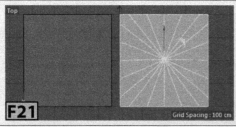 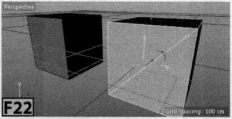

Untriangulate		U~U Shift+U	If you are importing a geometry built only of triangles, you can use this command to convert the triangles into quadrangles. You can specify the settings for this command from the **Untriangulate** dialog that opens when you click the gear icon located next to this command. The **Evaluate Angle** parameter in the dialog lets you specify the angle at which the resulting quad will be created between two triangles *Tip: Planar Qauds* *Try to use a value like **0.00001** for the **Evaluate Angle** parameter. When possible, CINEMA 4D will create planar quads using this value.*
Set Point Value		M~L	This command allows you to set values for the selected points. You can use this command to center points, quantize points, or crumple points.
Spin Edge			This command is used to spin the selected edges and then connect them to the neighboring two points, see Figure F23.

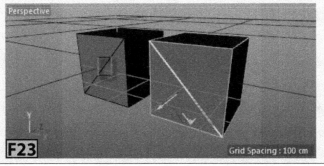

Edge to Spline		Use this command to create a spline from an edge selection, see Figure F24.

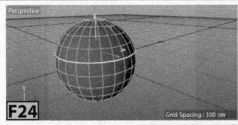 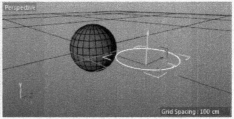

Change Point Order		A polygon is either a triangle or a quadrangle. A triangle has points A, B, and C whereas a quadrangle has four points A, B, C, and D. If these four points are not on the same plane, the quadrangle is a non-planar polygon. The **Change Point Order** command lets you change the order of the points of a polygon.

Optimize		U~O Shift+O	When you create objects using the **Connect Objects** command, very often, some points and surface would be duplicated in the resulting geometry. You can use this command to remove these points.
Reset Scale			You can use this command to restore the coordinate system of the object. You need to do this when the object's axes are not perpendicular to each other or have different lengths. Note that this type of issue occurs in CINEMA 4D's version prior to R12.
Modeling Settings			When you select this option, the **Modeling Settings** area appears in the **Attribute Manager**. From this section, you can specify various modeling settings such as **Snap** and **Quantize** settings.

Create Tools sub-menu

Create Point		M~A	This tool allows you to create new points to the objects. There is no need to make a selection and this tool works in all three modes. To add a point on an element, move the mouse pointer over the element, the element appears highlighted. Click on element to add the point. If you don't release the mouse button, you can drag the point to change its position on the element.
Polygon Pen		M~E	The **Polygon Pen** tool is a super tool, it is more than just a polygon painting tool. You can use it to edit the existing geometry as well as use it as a replacement for other tools/functions such as melting points, moving and duplicating elements, minor knife functions, extruding, tweaking, and so forth.
Edge Cut		M~F	This tool allows you to interactively subdivide the selected edges, see Figure F25. This tool works in the **Edges** mode only. You can also use the **Shift**, **Ctrl**, and **Ctrl+Shift** keys to adjust scale, offset, and subdivision, respectively. You can also set these properties numerically by specifying values for the **Offset**, **Scale**, and **Subdivision** parameters in the **Attribute Manager	Options** parameter group. When the **Create N-gons** switch in the **Options** parameter group is on, N-gons will be created else triangles will be created.

F25

Knife		M~K, K	This tool can be used to cut polygon and spline objects. It works in all three modes: **Points**, **Edges**, and **Polygons**. There are many options available in the **Options** parameter group to control the behavior of the **Knife** tool. Figure F26 shows an edge loop created using the **Loop** mode.

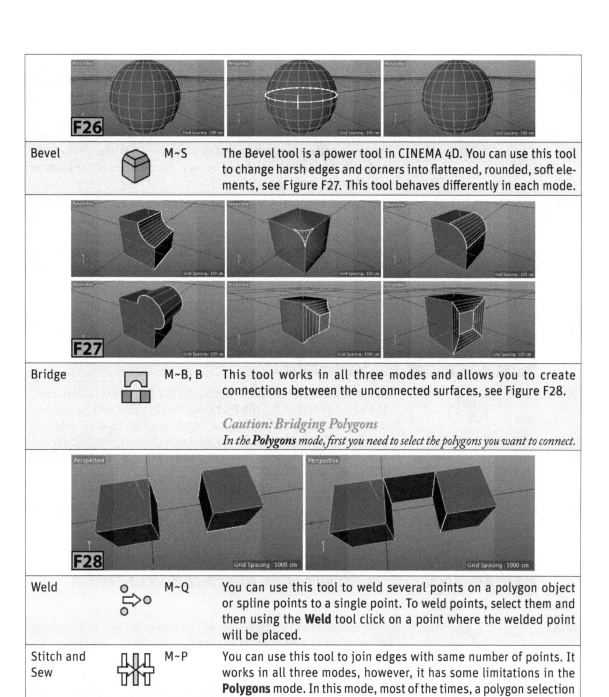

Bevel		M~S	The Bevel tool is a power tool in CINEMA 4D. You can use this tool to change harsh edges and corners into flattened, rounded, soft elements, see Figure F27. This tool behaves differently in each mode.
Bridge		M~B, B	This tool works in all three modes and allows you to create connections between the unconnected surfaces, see Figure F28. *Caution: Bridging Polygons* *In the **Polygons** mode, first you need to select the polygons you want to connect.*
Weld		M~Q	You can use this tool to weld several points on a polygon object or spline points to a single point. To weld points, select them and then using the **Weld** tool click on a point where the welded point will be placed.
Stitch and Sew		M~P	You can use this tool to join edges with same number of points. It works in all three modes, however, it has some limitations in the **Polygons** mode. In this mode, most of the times, a polygon selection is required.
Close Polygon Hole		M~D	This tool is used to fill a hole in a polygon mesh.

Extrude		M~T, D	This tool is used to extrude the selected points, edges, or polygons. If no elements are selected, it extrude the whole object. You can also interactively extrude in the viewport by dragging the mouse pointer to the left or right, see Figure F29.
Extrude Inner		M~W, I	The functioning of this tool is similar to that of the **Extrude** tool, however, you can extrude polygons inwards or outwards. The object shown in Figure F30 is created using a combination of the **Extrude** and **Extrude Inner** tools.
Matrix Extrude		M~X	The functioning of the **Matrix Extrude** tool is similar to the **Extrude** tool, but with one difference: you can make as many extrusion steps as you want in one step, see Figure F31. You can define the values for move, rotation, and size from the **Options** parameter group. You can also use **Shift**, **Ctrl**, and **Alt** to interactively set size, rotation, and directions values, respectively.

Smooth Shift		M~Y	The **Smooth Shift** tool works similar to the **Extrude** tool. However, the value specified for the **Maximum Angle** value will be used to determine if new connecting surface should be created between polygons. Figure F32 shows the initial selection of the polygons, and extruded polygons using **Maximum Angle** value of **71**, respectively.

Transform Tools sub-menu

Brush		M~C	This tool works in all three modes. This tool allows you to deform polygon mesh and paint/edit vertex maps. When you select this tool a sphere of influence appears in the editor view. All points inside the sphere will be affected by the tool. You can interactively change the size of the sphere by MMB dragging in the editor view to the left or to the right. To change strength, MMB drag vertically.
Iron		M~G	This tool behaves like a virtual iron and lets you smooth the uneven surfaces. The strength of the iron is controlled using the **Percent** value in the **Options** parameter group.

Magnet		M~I	You can use this tool to pull sections out of polygons or spline objects.
Mirror		M~H	You can use this tool to mirror points and polygons. It can also be applied on the splines. It works only in the **Points** and **Polygons** modes. You can also define mirroring axis interactively. To define the axis, click and drag in the editor view.
Slide		M~O	This tool is used to move selected edges, and edge loops vertically outwards or inwards. To offset the edges, activate this tool and slide the selected edges. You can use the **Ctrl** key to create copy of selected edges. The **Shift** key is used to push edges inwards or outwards.
Normal Move		M~Z	This interactive tool allows you to move the selected polygons in the direction of their normals. It works only in the **Polygons** mode.
Normal Scale		M~#	This interactive tool allows you to scale the selected polygons in the direction of their normals. It works only in the **Polygons** mode.
Normal Rotate		M~,	This interactive tool allows you to rotate the selected polygons in the direction of their normals. It works only in the **Polygons** mode.
Weight Subdivision Surface		M~R	This tool is used with the **Subdivisions Surface** objects. You can use it to weight subdivision surfaces.
N-Gons sub-menu			
N-gon Triangulation		U~T	While rendering and animating n-gons, CINEMA 4D triangulates them internally. If you want to preview them in the viewport, turn on the **N-gon Lines** switch from the **Viewport Settings	Filter** parameter group. The **N-gon Triangulation** command is a toggle switch. When on, an n-gon will be internally retriangulated each time you move any n-gon's points. When off, you can triangulate the n-gons manually by using command available in the **Mesh	N-gons** sub-menu.
Retriangulate N-gons		U~G	See the **N-gon Triangulation** description.
Remove N-gons		U~E	This command can be used to convert the selected objects' n-gons to triangles and quadrangles.
Normals sub-menu			
Align Normals		U~A	You can use this command to adjust and re-align the incorrect surface normals to the correct direction. The normals are used by CINEMA 4D to recognize an object's inner and outer surfaces.

Reverse Normals		U~R	You can use this command to reverse the normals of the object.
Break Phong Shading			Use this command to break the phong shading.
Unbreak Phong Shading			You can use this command to restore the phong shading.
Select Broken Phong Edges			This command selects all broken phong edges.

Axis Center sub-menu

Axis Center		This tool is used to quickly specify the object axis of a polygonal object. Choose this tool to open the **Axis Center** dialog box. Set options in this dialog and then click **Execute** to set the object axis.
Center Axis to		The object axis will be moved but no geometry.
Center Object to		The object geometry will be moved along the axis.
Center Parent to		The object axis of the parent object of the object selected in the **Object Manager** and its corresponding geometry will be moved onto the selected object.
Center to Parent		The selected object's axis and its corresponding geometry will be placed onto the parent object.
View Center		The object axis and the corresponding geometry will be moved to the center of the view.

Spline sub-menu

Hard Interpolation		This command changes all selected points to hard interpolation. If no points are selected, all points on the spline are changed to hard interpolation, see Figure F33. When you execute this command, CINEMA 4D essentially sets the length of the tangents to **0**.
Soft Interpolation		This command changes all selected points to soft interpolation, see Figure F34.
Equal Tangent Length		When you execute this command, the shorter tangent handle is set to the length to that of the second associated tangent, see Figure F35.

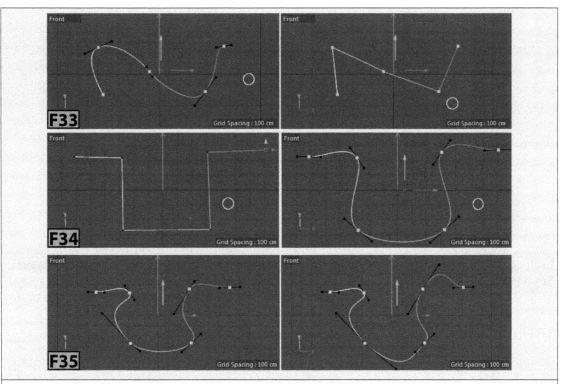

Equal Tangent Direction		This command is used to restore the smoothness of the broken tangents, see Figure F36.

Tip: Breaking Tangents
*You can use the **Move** tool with the **Shift** key to break the tangent's handles association and move one tangent handle while leaving the other unchanged.*

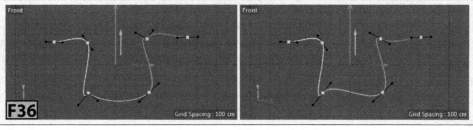

Join Segment		You can use this command to connect several unconnected segments. To connect segments, select one or more points of each segment and then use the **Join Segment** command, see Figure F37.
Break Segment		This command is used to create a new spline segment. To break spline, select one of the points and execute this command, a new segment appears and all points on either side of the separated segment will become a new segment, see Figure F38. Note that this command works in the **Points** mode only.

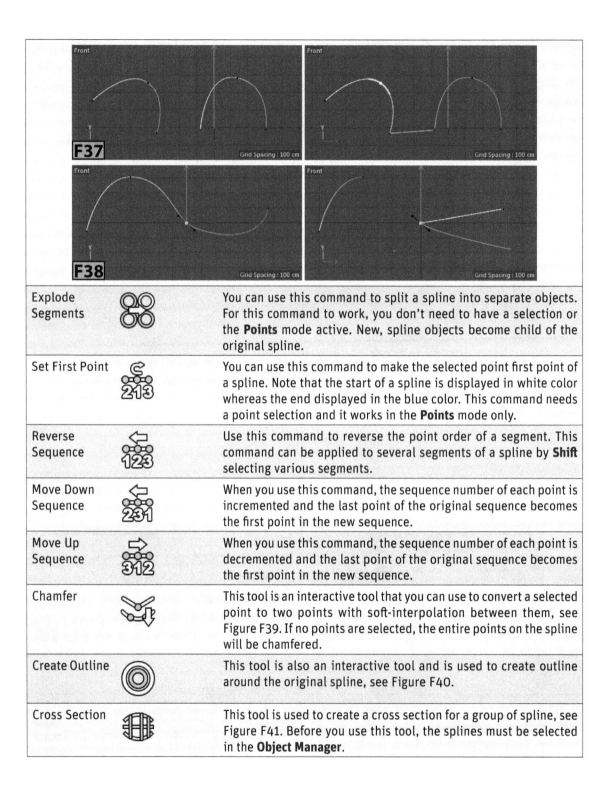

Explode Segments		You can use this command to split a spline into separate objects. For this command to work, you don't need to have a selection or the **Points** mode active. New, spline objects become child of the original spline.
Set First Point		You can use this command to make the selected point first point of a spline. Note that the start of a spline is displayed in white color whereas the end displayed in the blue color. This command needs a point selection and it works in the **Points** mode only.
Reverse Sequence		Use this command to reverse the point order of a segment. This command can be applied to several segments of a spline by **Shift** selecting various segments.
Move Down Sequence		When you use this command, the sequence number of each point is incremented and the last point of the original sequence becomes the first point in the new sequence.
Move Up Sequence		When you use this command, the sequence number of each point is decremented and the last point of the original sequence becomes the first point in the new sequence.
Chamfer		This tool is an interactive tool that you can use to convert a selected point to two points with soft-interpolation between them, see Figure F39. If no points are selected, the entire points on the spline will be chamfered.
Create Outline		This tool is also an interactive tool and is used to create outline around the original spline, see Figure F40.
Cross Section		This tool is used to create a cross section for a group of spline, see Figure F41. Before you use this tool, the splines must be selected in the **Object Manager**.

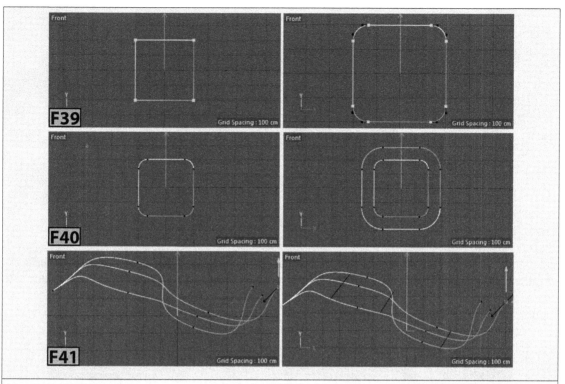

| Line Up | | Use this command to align sequentially selected points to a straight line, see Figure F42. |

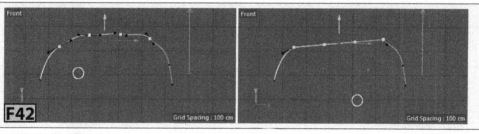

| Project | | You can use this command to project a spline onto surfaces of the other objects, see Figure F43. To understand the working of this command, create a sphere and helix. Make helix spline primitive editable. Execute the **Project** command. From the **Options** parameter group in the **Attribute Manager**, select **Spherical** from the **Mode** drop-down and then from the **Tool** parameter group, click **Apply**. |
| Round | | You can use this command to round and subdivide the sequentially selected points of a spline, see Figure F44. |

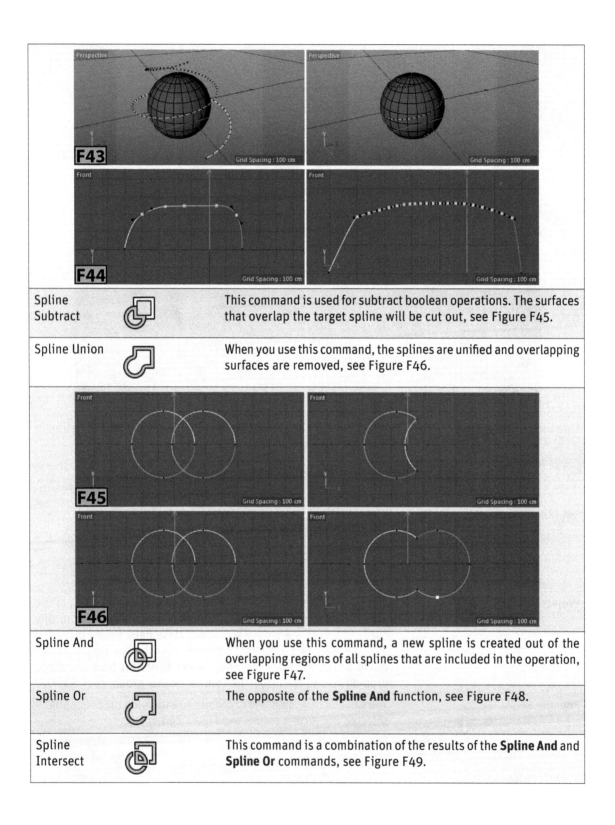

Spline Subtract		This command is used for subtract boolean operations. The surfaces that overlap the target spline will be cut out, see Figure F45.
Spline Union		When you use this command, the splines are unified and overlapping surfaces are removed, see Figure F46.

Spline And		When you use this command, a new spline is created out of the overlapping regions of all splines that are included in the operation, see Figure F47.
Spline Or		The opposite of the **Spline And** function, see Figure F48.
Spline Intersect		This command is a combination of the results of the **Spline And** and **Spline Or** commands, see Figure F49.

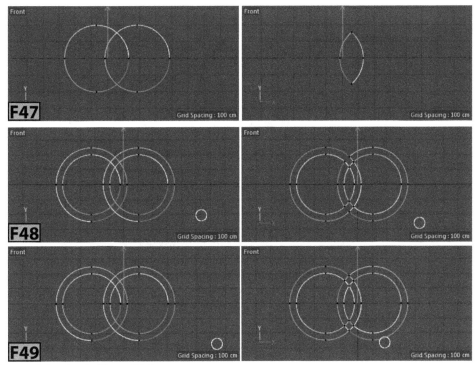

Working with Modeling Objects

CINEMA 4D offers several modeling functions that provide some special modeling features. You can access them from the **Modeling Objects** sub-menu of the **Create** menu. You can also access them from the **Modeling Objects** command group of the **Standard** palette, see Figure F50. Following table summarizes the function available in the **Modeling Objects** command group.

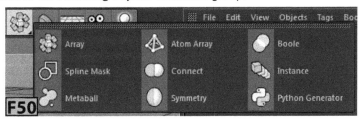

Table 3: The functions available in the **Modeling Objects** command group

Function	Icon	Description
Array		This function is used to create copies of an object. The copied objects can be arranged in a spherical or wave form and are placed around the origin of the array object, see Figure F51. The amplitude of the wave can be animated. The object you want to copy must be child of the array.
Atom Array		You can use the **Atom Array** function to create atomic lattice structure from the child objects. When you apply this function, all edges are replaced with the cylinders and points are replaced with the spheres, see Figure F52.

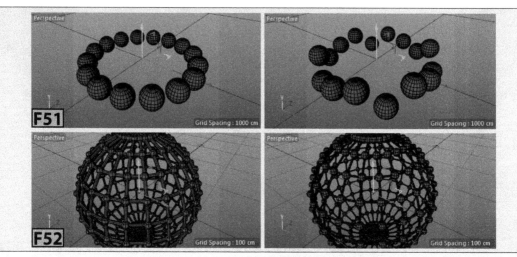

Boole	This function is used to apply boolean operations on the primitives or polygons, see Figure F53. You can also use this function on hierarchies. The two objects on which you want to apply this function should be children of the **Boole** object. The default operation for this function is A subtract B. Therefore, the order of the child objects is important. *Note: Boolean Operations* *You need to make sure the objects to which you want to apply this function should have closed volume and cleanly structured otherwise unwanted results may occur. Also, note that the higher the subdivisions of the objects, cleaner the cut will be.*

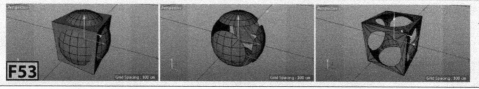

Spline Mask	This function is used to apply boolean operations on the splines. This function produces best results when splines are smooth and all are in the same plane, see Figure F54. *Tip: Spline in Polygons Mode* *You can display a closed booled spline shape in the **Polygons** mode, see the right image in Figure F54, by making it editable by pressing **C** or using the **Current State to Object** command from the **Mesh** menu. To this to work, you need to turn on the **Create Cap** switch from the **Spline Mask's Object** parameter group.*
Connect	This function combines separate objects using a defined tolerance. It also gives you ability to weld them together, see Figure F55. To use this function, select all the objects that you want to connect and then press **Alt+G** to group them under a **Null** object and then make **Null** child of the **Connect Object**. To smooth the connections, you can use a **Subdivision Surface** object.

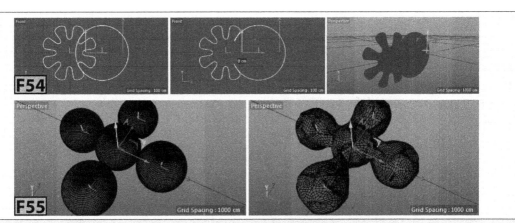

Instance		You can use this function to create instances of an object. An instance does not have its own geometry and it takes far less memory than the copied geometries. However, **MoGraph's Cloner Object** is much more powerful than the **Instance** Object.
Metaball		This function creates an elastic skin over the spline and spline objects. You can use parametric objects, splines, and polygon objects with this function, see Figures F56 and F57.

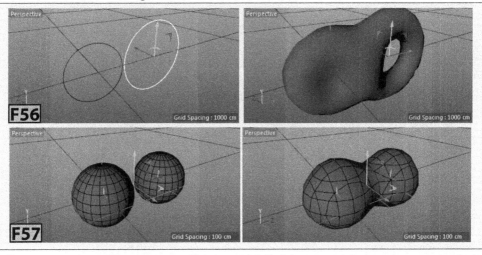

Symmetry Object		If you are creating a model that is symmetric in nature, you only have to model half the model. The other half you can generate using this function. Only the part on which you applied this function will have the points. If you manipulate these points, the action will be reflected in the other part as well.
Python Generator		This function is used to enter **Python** code which can be used to generate the geometry.

Exploring Deformers

The deformer objects in CINEMA 4D are used primarily to deform the shape of the primitive objects, Generator objects, polygon objects and splines, see Figure F58. Unlike the **Generators** and **Modeling Objects**, deformers act as children of their parents. A deformer will have no effect on the geometry if it is at the top of the hierarchy. To add a deformer, select the parent object in the **Object Manager**, hold **Shift** and then choose the desired deformer from the **Standard Palette | Deformer Objects** command group, see Figure F59. You can apply multiple deformers on the same object.

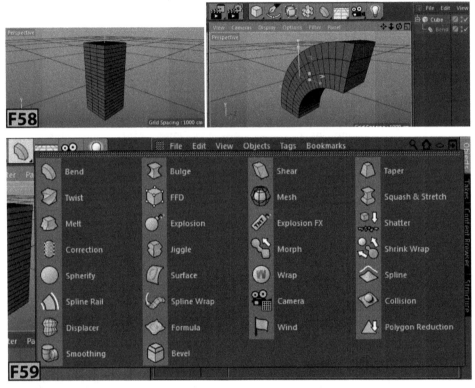

Caution: Deformer Object

*The **Deformer Object** does not work in conjunction with the following functions in CINEMA 4D: **Explosion Object**, **ExplosionFX**, **Polygon Reduction**, **Spline Deformer**; and **Shatter Object**.*

The following table summarizes the deformer objects available in CINEMA 4D.

Table 4: The deformer objects available in the CINEMA 4D		
Function	**Icon**	**Description**
Bend		This deformer bends an object. You can drag the orange handle on the deformer surface to interactively control the amount of bend.
Bulge		Use this deformer to make an object bulge or contract. You can drag the orange handle on the deformer surface to interactively control the amount of bulge.

Shear		It shears an object.
Taper		It tapers [narrows or widens towards on end] an object.
Twist		It twists an object around its Y-axis. For smooth twist, ensure there are sufficient number of subdivisions along the twist axis.
FFD		This deformer deforms objects using a grid points. This deformer works in the **Points** mode only.
Mesh Deformer		This deformer somewhat works like the **FFD** deformer. You can use it to create a custom low-res cage around the model and then deform freely.
Squash and Stretch		This modifier allows to produce the squash and stretch effect that you see in the bouncing ball animation.
Melt		Use this deformer to melt the object radially from origin [Y plane] of the deformer.
Explosion		This deformer lets you explode an object to its constituent polygons. To animate the explosion, animate the **Strength** parameter.
ExplosionFX		Use this deformer to quickly create and animate realistic explosion effects.
Shatter		Use this deformer to shatter objects into individual polygons which then fall to the ground plane.
Correction		This deformer allows you to access the points in their deformed state and then allows you change the positon of these points in the deformed state.
Jiggle		You can use this deformer to create secondary motion for a character's motion.
Morph		This deformer lets you blend in the morph targets within the region of influence of the deformer.
Shrink Wrap		This deformer allows you to shrink wrap the source object onto the target object.
Spherify		You can use this modifier to deform an object into a spherical shape.

Surface		Use this deformer to make an object follow the surface deformations of another object.
Wrap		You can use this modifier to wrap flat surface onto a curved surface.
Spline Deformer		This deformer takes two splines: original spline and modifying spline. It considers the difference in the position and shape of the two splines and then deforms the object accordingly.
Spline Rail		It deforms the polygon objects using upto four splines. These splines define the target shape.
Spline Wrap		This deformer allows you to deform an object along a spline.
Camera Deformer		You can use this deformer to deform an object based on the grid overplayed on the camera view.
Collision Deformer		This deformer deforms the objects using the collision interaction. You can think it as if a soft surface being pulled or pushed when it collides with another surface.
Displacer		This modifier allows you to create effects like created by the displacement mapping.
Formula		You can use this deformer and a mathematical formula to deform objects.
Wind Deform		Use this deformer to create waves on an object. The effect of this deformer will be along the deformer's positive X direction.
Polygon Reduction		This deformer allows you to reduce the number of polygons of an object.
Smoothing Deformer		Use this deformer to smooth the surface it is affecting.
Bevel		The functioning of this deformer is almost similar to the **Bevel** tool.

Hands-on Exercises

Before you start the hands-on exercises, let's first create a project folder that will host the exercise files. Open the **Windows Explorer** and navigate to the folder **c4dr17studio** in the **C** drive of your system. Create a sub-folder with the name **unit-cm2** in the **c4dr17studio** folder.

Exercise 1: Creating a Serving Bowl

In this exercise, you will create model of a bowl [see Figure E1].

E1

The following table summarizes the exercise:

Table E1: Creating a Serving Bowl	
Skill level	Beginner
Time to complete	20 Minutes
Topics in the section	• Getting Started • Creating the Bowl
Project Folder	c4dr17studio/unit-cm2
Units	Centimeters
Final exercise file	ucm2-hoe1-end.c4d

Getting Started

Start a new scene in CINEMA 4D and set units to **Centimeters**.

Creating the Bowl

Click **Cylinder** ⬡ from **SP | Object** CG to create a cylinder in the editor view. Rename **Cylinder** as **bowlGeo** in **OM**. In **AM | bowlGeo | Object** PG, set **Radius** to **25.591**, **Height** to **13**, and **Height Segments** to **2**. Press **O** to frame the object in the editor view. Press **NB** to enable the **Gouraud Shading (Lines)** mode, see Figure E2. Press **C** to make **bowlGeo** editable and then activate the **Points** mode. Select the top point, see Figure E3, and then press **Delete** to remove top part of **bowlGeo**.

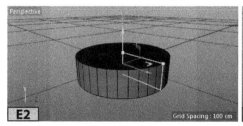

E2

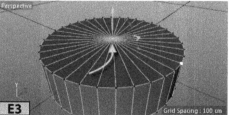

E3

Now, select the bottom point, see Figure E4, and then press **UZ** to melt the point to get a plane surface, see Figure E5. Now, if you move any of the bottom points using the **Move** ✛ tool, you would notice that these cap points are not connected with the rest of the geometry. Now, we will fix it.

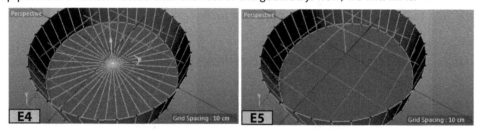

Undo the move operation, if any and then click **Connect** ⬭ from the **Generator** CG with **Alt** held down to add make the **Connect** object parent of **bowlGeo**. In **AM | Connect | Object** PG, select **Manual** from the **Phong Mode** drop-down. Ensure **Connect** is selected in **OM** and then press **C** to convert it to a polygonal object.

What just happened?
*The **Connect** generator connects the points of the cap section to the rest of the geometry. Notice in **AM**, the **Weld** switch is on. When on, CINEMA 4D welds the points using a tolerance value specified using the **Tolerance** parameter. Then, I converted the **Connect** object to an editable polygon object for farther changing the shape of the bowl.*

Now, activate the **Polygons** 🔶 mode. Select the bottom polygon, see Figure E6, and then **Ctrl+click** on **TP | Points** 🔶 to select the bottom points, refer to Figure E7. In **CM**, enter **40** in the **Size X** and **Size Z** fields to scale the points, see Figure E8.

Note: Live Selection tool
*Press and hold the **9** key to temporarily enable the **Live Selection** tool.*

Activate the **Polygons** mode and then select the bottom polygon. Press **MT** to enable the **Extrude** 🔶 tool and then in **AM | Extrude | Options** PG, enter **1** in the **Offset** field to extrude the polygon, see Figure E9. You can also extrude polygon interactively in the editor view by dragging the mouse pointer to the left or right.

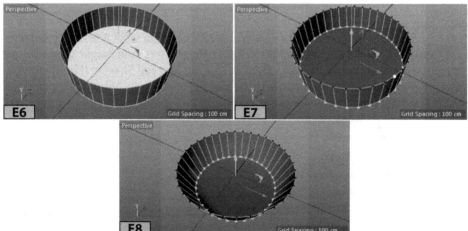

Press **MW** to enable the **Extrude Inner** 🔶 tool and then enter **1** in **AM | Extrude Inner | Options** PG | **Offset** field to extrude the polygon, see Figure E10. **Ctrl+click** on **TP | Points** to select the points associated with the previously selected polygon. Press **UC** to collapse the points, see Figure E11. Activate the **Polygons** mode and then press **Ctrl+A** to select all polygons.

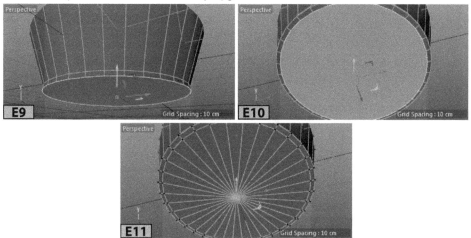

Press **MT** to enable the **Extrude** tool and then in **AM | Extrude | Options** PG, enter **1** in the **Offset** field to give thickness to the bowl, see Figure E12. In **OM**, rename **Connect** as **bowlGeo**. Press **UL** to select the **Loop Selection** tool and then select the loops, in the **Edges** mode, as shown in Figure E13. Press **MS** to activate the **Bevel** tool and then in **AM | Bevel | Tool Option** PG, set **Offset** to **0.1** and **Subdivision** to **1** to chamfer the edges, see Figure E14. Similarly, chamfer the bottom and inner edges, see Figure E15.

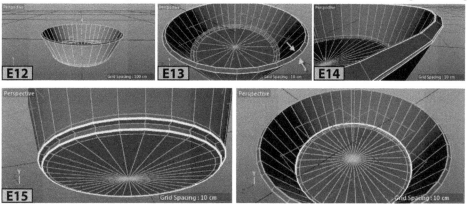

What just happened?
I have added some edge loops at the top and bottom of the bowl. It will help us to retain the shape of the bowl when we will apply smoothing to it.

Activate the **Model** mode form the **TP**. Now, choose **Taper** from the **Deformer** CG with **Shift** held down to make the **Taper** object child of **bowlGeo**. In **AM | Taper | Object** PG, set **Size X** to **25**, **Mode** to **Within Box**, and **Strength** to **-15%**, see Figure E16. In **OM**, create a copy of **Taper** object, see Figure E17 and then enter **90** in **CM | Rotation H** field, see Figure E18. Ensure **Taper.1** is selected in **OM** and then **AM | Taper | Object** PG, set **Size Z** to **70**, see Figure E19. Ensure **bowlGeo** is selected in **OM** and then choose **Subdivision Surface** from **SP | Generator** CG with **Alt** held down to smooth the object.

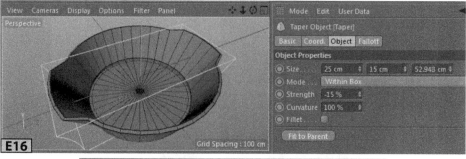

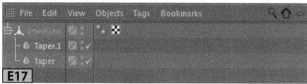

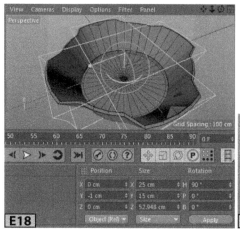

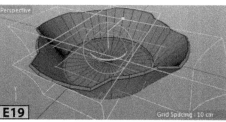

Exercise 2: Creating a Kitchen Cabinet

In this exercise, you will create model of a kitchen cabinet [see Figure E1].

The following table summarizes the exercise:

Table E2: Creating a Kitchen Cabinet	
Skill level	Beginner
Time to complete	20 Minutes
Topics in the section	• Getting Started • Creating the Cabinet
Project Folder	c4dr17studio/unit-cm2
Units	Centimeters
Final exercise file	ucm2-hoe2-end.c4d

Getting Started
Start a new scene in CINEMA 4D and set units to **Centimeters**.

Creating the Cabinet
Choose **Cube** from **SP | Object** CG to create a cube in the editor view. Rename **Cube** as **cabinetGeo** in OM. In **AM | cabinetGeo | Object** PG, set **Size X** to **38**, **Size Y** to **76**, and **Size Z** to **45**. Press **O** to frame the object in the editor view. Press **NB** to enable the **Gouraud Shading (Lines)** mode, see Figure E2. Press **C** to make **cabinetGeo** editable.

Select the top and bottom polygons of the **cabinetGeo** and then press **UP** to split the polygons.

What just happened?
*Here, I've applied the **Split** function on the selected polygons. As a result, CINEMA 4D creates a new object from the selected polygons leaving the original geometry unchanged, see Figure E3.*

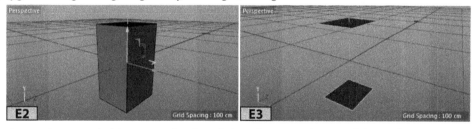

Rename the newly created object as **topbotGeo**. Select the two polygons of the **topbotGeo** and then press **MT** to enable the **Extrude** tool and then in **AM | Extrude | Options** PG, enter **3** in the **Offset** field to extrude the polygon, see Figure E4. Now, select the polygon, see Figure E5, and then move it by **3** units in the negative Z direction using the **Move** tool, see Figure E6.

Select the top polygon and then extrude the polygon by **5** units using the **Extrude** tool, see Figure E7. Now, select the polygon shown in Figure E8 and extrude it by **5** units along the positive Z direction, see Figure E9. Select the edges of **cabinetGeo**, refer Figure E29, and then press **Alt+X** to connect the edges, see Figure E10. Select the polygons, see Figure E11, and then press **MW** to activate the **Extrude Inner** 🔲 tool. In **AM | Extrude Inner | Options** PG, turn off the **Preserve Groups** switch and then set **Offset** to **2**, see Figure F12. Now, select the newly created polygons and then extrude them by **2.5** units, see Figure E13. Now, select all the outer hard edges and apply little chamfering to them using the **Bevel** tool, as done in Exercise 1, see Figure E14.

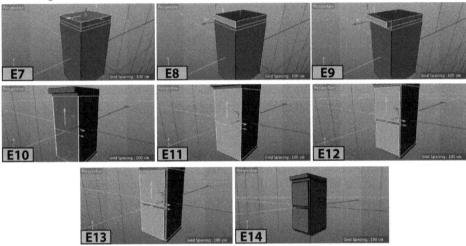

Exercise 3: Creating a Book

In this exercise, you will create model of a book [see Figures E1 and E2].

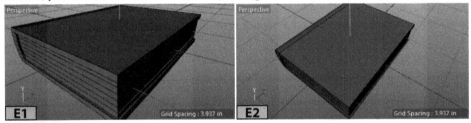

The following table summarizes the exercise:

Table E3: Creating a Book	
Skill level	Beginner
Time to complete	20 Minutes
Topics in the section	• Getting Started • Creating the Book
Project Folder	c4dr17studio/unit-cm2
Units	Inches
Final exercise file	ucm2-hoe3-end.c4d

Getting Started
Start a new scene in CINEMA 4D and set units to **Inches**.

Creating the Book
Choose **Cube** from **SP | Object** CG to create a cube in the editor view. Rename **Cube** as **bookGeo** in **OM**. In **AM | bookGeo | Object** PG, set **Size X** to **7.44**, **Size Y** to **2**, and **Size Z** to **9.69**. Press **O** to frame the object in the editor view. Press **NB** to enable the **Gouraud Shading (Lines)** mode, see Figure E3. Press **C** to make **cabinetGeo** editable.

Press **UB** to activate the **Ring Selection** ⬚ tool and then select the edge ring, refer Figure E4. Press **Alt+X** to connect the edges. Select the newly created edge loop by double-clicking on it using the **Move** tool and then slide it towards the negative X axis, see Figure E5. Select the edge ring using the **Ring Selection** tool, see Figure E6. Press **Alt+X** thrice to create new edge loops, see Figure E7. Select the polygons that will make pages of the book, see Figure E8.

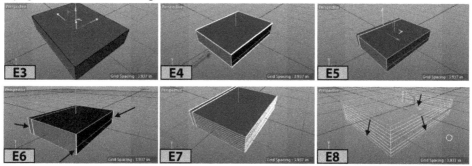

Press **MT** to enable the **Extrude** tool and then in **AM | Extrude | Options** PG, enter **-0.1** in the **Offset** field and **180** in the **Maximum Angle** field to extrude the polygons inwards, see Figure E9. In the **Front** view, select the points shown in Figure E10. Make sure the **Only Select Visible Elements** switch is off in **AM**. Move the points, as shown in Figure E11.

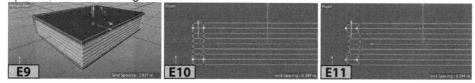

Similarly, move other points to make shape of the book, see Figure E12. Select the outer edges of the book, see Figure E13 and then bevel the edges using the **Bevel** tool. Press **MS** to activate the **Bevel** tool and then in **AM | Bevel | Tool Option** PG, set **Offset** to **0.01** and **Subdivision** to **2** to chamfer the edges, see Figure E14.

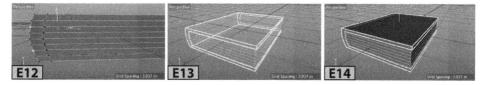

Exercise 4: Creating a Waste Bin

In this exercise, you will create model of a waste bin [see Figure E1].

E1

The following table summarizes the exercise:

Table E4: Creating a Waste Bin	
Skill level	Beginner
Time to complete	30 Minutes
Topics in the section	• Getting Started • Creating the Bin
Project Folder	c4dr17studio/unit-cm2
Units	Inches
Final exercise file	ucm2-hoe4-end.c4d

Getting Started

Start a new scene in CINEMA 4D and set units to **Inches**.

Creating the Bin

Choose **Cylinder** from **SP | Object** CG. In **AM | Cylinder | Object** PG, set **Radius** to **15**, **Height** to **45**, **Height Segments** to **30**, and **Rotation Segments** to **50**. Press **NB** to enable **Gouroud Shading (Lines)** display mode. Press **C** to make **Cylinder** editable. Press **UB** to activate the **Ring Selection** tool and click at the top of the cylinder to select polygons. Press **Delete** to remove the top polygons, see Figure E2. Press **UL** to activate the **Loop Selection** tool and then select top and bottom rows of polygons using **Shift**, see Figure E3.

E2 E3

Press **MT** to enable the **Extrude** tool and then in **AM | Extrude | Options** PG, set **Offset** to **1.2**, see Figure E4. Ensure the newly extruded polygons are selected and then press **MS** to activate the **Bevel** tool. In **AM | Bevel | Tool Option** PG, set **Offset** to **0.6**. In the **AM | Bevel | Polygon Extrusion** PG, set **Extrusion** to **0.6** see Figure E5.

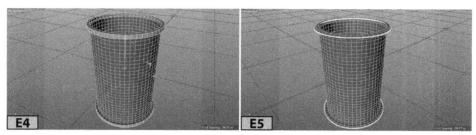

Press **UB** to activate the **Ring Selection** tool and then select every alternate column of polygons using **Shift**, see Figure E6. Activate the **Rectangle Selection** ⬜ tool from the **Selection** CG and then in **AM**, turn off the **Only Select Visible Elements** switch. In the **Front** view, remove two top and bottom loops of polygons using **Ctrl**, see Figure E7.

Press **MT** to enable the **Extrude** tool and then in **AM | Extrude | Options** PG, set **Offset** to **-0.5**, see Figure E8. Press **NA** to enable the **Gouroud Shading** display mode. Hold **Alt** and then choose **Subdivision Surface** from the **Generator** CG to make the cylinder smooth, see Figure E9. In **OM**, rename **Subdivision Surface** as **Waste Bin**. Next, you will create a lid for the cylinder.

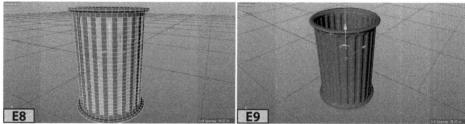

Choose **Cylinder** from **SP | Object** CG. In **AM | Cylinder | Object** PG, set **Radius** to **17**, **Height** to **2**, **Height Segments** to **1**, and **Rotation Segments** to **50**. Press **NB** to enable **Gouroud Shading (Lines)** display mode. Rename **Cylinder** as **Lid** in **OM** and then press **C** to make it editable. Press **UB** to activate the **Ring Selection** tool and click at the bottom of the **Lid** to select bottom polygons. Press **MW** to select the **Extrude Inner** tool and then in **AM | Extrude Inner | Options** PG, set **Offset** to **1**, see Figure E10. Now, using **Extrude** tool extrude the polygons by setting **Offset** to **-1** in **AM**, see Figure E11.

Select all points of the **Lid** in the **Points** mode and then press **UO** to optimize the **Lid**.

What just happened?
*I have welded the points of the cap of the **Lid** with rest of geometry using the **Optimize** function. Now, when I will apply the **Bevel** tool in up next, the whole geometry will remain intact.*

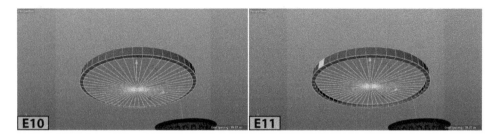

Select the edges loops shown in Figure E12 and then press **MS** to activate the **Bevel** tool. In **AM** | **Bevel** | **Tool Option** PG, set **Offset** to **0.2** and **Subdivision** to **2**, see Figure E13.

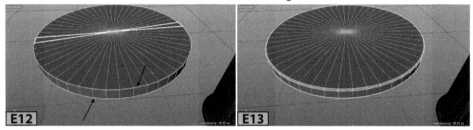

Using the **Ring Selection** tool, select the top polygons of the **Lid** and then press **MW** to select the **Extrude Inner** tool and then **in AM** | **Extrude Inner** | **Options** PG, set **Offset** to **9.5**, see Figure E14. Activate the **Move** tool and then move the selected polygon in the positive Y direction by **1** unit, see Figure E15. Press **NA** to enable the **Gouroud Shading** display mode and then align the **Lid** on top of the **Waste Bin**, see Figure E16. Now, you will create handle for the **Lid**.

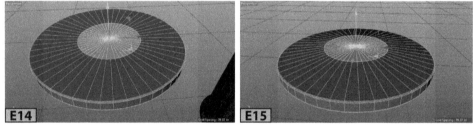

Choose **Torus** ⊙ from **SP** | **Object** CG. In **AM** | **Torus** | **Object** PG, set **Ring Radius** to **4.64**, **Ring Segments** to **50**, **Pipe Radius** to **0.84**, and **Pipe Segments** to **36** and then align it with the **Lid**, see Figure E17. Rename **Torus** as **Handle** in **OM**.

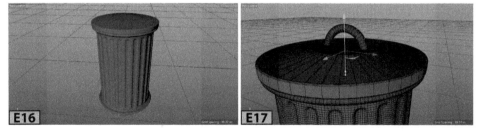

Exercise 5: Creating a Desk

In this exercise, you will create model of a waste bin [see Figure E1].

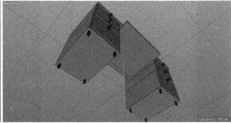

The following table summarizes the exercise:

Table E5: Creating a Waste Bin	
Skill level	Beginner
Time to complete	30 Minutes
Topics in the section	• Getting Started • Creating the Desk
Project Folder	c4dr17studio/unit-cm2
Units	Inches
Final exercise file	ucm2-hoe5-end.c4d

Getting Started

Start a new scene in CINEMA 4D and set units to **Centimeters**.

Creating the Bin

Choose **Cube** from **SP | Object** CG to create a cube in the editor view. In **AM | Cube | Object** PG, set **Size X** to **60**, **Size Y** to **2.5**, and **Size Z** to **150**. Press **O** to frame the object in the editor view. Press **NB** to enable the **Gouraud Shading (Lines)** mode. Create another cube and then in **AM | Cube.1 | Object** PG, set **Size X** to **60**, **Size Y** to **62**, and **Size Z** to **40**, see Figure E2.

Select **Cube** and **Cube.1** in **OM** and then choose **Arrange Objects | Center** from the **Tools** menu. In **AM | Center | Options** PG, select **Negative** from the **Y Axis** and **Z Axis** drop-downs. Click **Apply** from the **Tool** PG. Click **New Transform** from the **Tool** PG and then in the **Options** PG, select **Positive** from the **Y Axis** drop-down to align the cubes, see Figure E3. Now, using the **Move** tool align the two cubes as shown in Figure E4.

Ensure **Cube.1** selected in **OM** and then choose **Arrange Objects | Duplicate** from the **Tools** menu. In **AM | Duplicate | Duplicate** PG, set **Copies** to **1**. In the **Options** PG, select **Linear** from the **Mode** drop-down. In the **Position** section, set **Move X, Move Y,** and **Move Z** to **0, 0,** and **110**, respectively to align the duplicate to the other end of the table top, see Figure E5.

What just happened?
*Here, I've created a duplicate of the **Cube.1** using the **Duplicate** command and then offset it by **110** [150–40=110] units along the positive Z axis.*

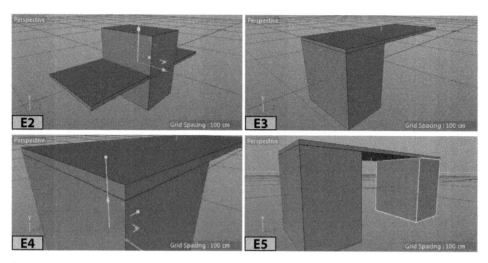

Press **Ctrl+A** to select all cubes and then press **C** to make them editable. Now, choose **Conversion | Connect Objects + Delete** from the **Mesh** menu. Rename the unified geometry as **deskGeo** in **OM**.

What just happened?
I've made all thee cube primitives editable and then combined the result in a single unified polygon object.

Press **UB** to activate the **Ring Selection** tool and then select the edges [in the **Edges** mode] of the bases of the table using **Shift**, see Figure E6. Press **Alt+X** to connect the edges, see Figure E7. Now, select the top rings of the bases, see Figure E8, and then press **Alt+X** to connect the edges, see Figure E9.

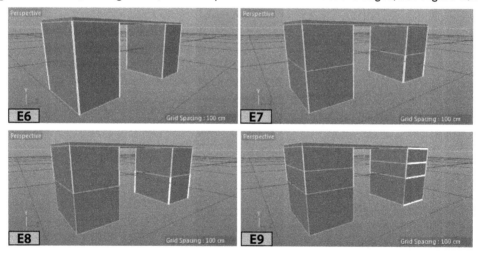

Select the polygons shown in Figure E10. Press **MW** to select the **Extrude Inner** tool and then in **AM | Extrude Inner | Options** PG, turn off the **Preserve Groups** switch and then set **Offset** to **1.5**, see Figure E11. Press **MT** to enable the **Extrude** tool and then in **AM | Extrude | Options** PG, set **Offset** to **1.5**, see Figure E12.

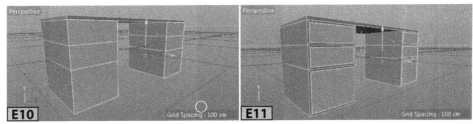

Now, we'll create keyboard support. For that we will place some edges using the **Knife** tool. Activate the **Right** viewport and then press **MK** to activate the **Knife** tool. In **AM | Knife | Options** section, select **Plane** from the **Mode** drop-down and **X-Z** from the **Plane** drop-down. Now, click to create an edge loop, click again to create another loop, see Figure E13.

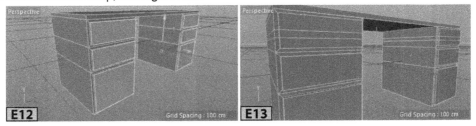

Now, select the polygons shown in Figure E14 and press **UP** to split the polygons. Rename the new geometry is **keyboardGeo** in **OM**. Select the newly created polygons and press **MB** to activate the **Bridge** tool. In **AM | Bridge | Options** section, turn off the **Delete Original Polygons** switch and then click on one of the polygons to make a bridge between them, see Figure E15. Now, switch to the **Model** mode and pull out the keyboard little bit using the **Move** tool, see Figure E16.

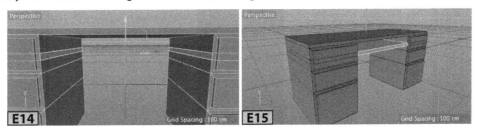

Press **Ctrl+A** to select all objects in **OM** and then choose **Conversion | Connect Objects + Delete** from the **Mesh** menu. Rename the unified geometry as **deskGeo** in **OM**.

Note: Cleaning the Model
You can remove the edges that we added for creating the keyboard support by first selecting them and then using the ***Dissolve*** *command.*

Select the polygon shown in Figure E17 and then press **MT** to enable the **Extrude** tool and then in **AM | Extrude | Options** PG, set **Offset** to **2.5**, see Figure E18. In **Edges** mode, press **Ctrl+A** to select all edges and then press **MS** to activate the **Bevel** tool. In **AM | Bevel | Tool Option** PG, set **Offset** to **0.1** and **Subdivision** to **2**, see Figure E19.

Now, we'll create knobs for the drawers using a cylinder. Choose **Cylinder** from **SP | Object** CG. In **AM | Cylinder | Object** PG, set **Radius** to **1.5**, **Height** to **6**, and **Rotation Segments** to **18**. In the **Caps** PG, turn on the **Fillet** switch and then set **Segments** to **3** and **Radius** to **0.074**. Press **C** to make the cylinder editable. Select the edge ring, shown in Figure E20 and then press **Alt+X** to connect the edges, see Figure E21.

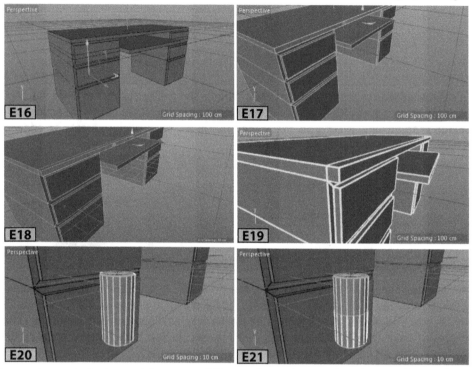

Select the newly created edge and then press **MS** to activate the **Bevel** tool. In **AM | Bevel | Tool Option** PG, set **Offset** to **0.02** and **Subdivisions** to **0**, see Figure E22. **Ctrl+click** on **Polygons** in **TP** to select the newly created polygons. Now, interactively inset and extrude the polygons using the **Extrude Inner** and **Extrude** tools, respectively, see Figure E23.

Ensure **Cylinder** is selected in **OM** and then choose **Subdivision Surface** from the **Generator** CG with **Alt** held down to smooth the cylinder. Now, create copies of the cylinder to align them with drawers of the desk, see Figure E24. Similarly, create legs of the desk, see Figure E25.

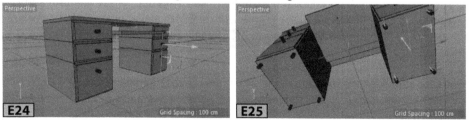

Practical Tests

Test 1: Creating a Flash Drive

Create a model of flash drive using polygon modeling techniques [see Figure P1].

Hint Test - 1

*Set **Units** to **Millimeters**. Create a **Cylinder** primitive and then set its **Radius** to 7.5, **Height** to 7, **Height Segments** to 1, and **Rotation Segments** to 36. Make it editable and then dissolve the top and bottom points using the **Dissolve** command, see Figure P2. Weld the points using the **Connect** object, as done in **Exercise -1**. Select the one half of the points in the **Top** view and then move them about 25 units to the right see Figure P3. Now, use various modeling tools and functions to create the flash drive model.*

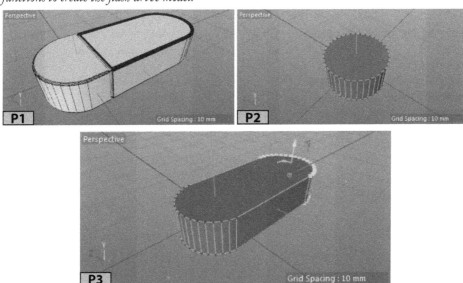

Test 2: Creating a USB Connector

Create a model of USB connector using polygon modeling techniques [see Figure P4].

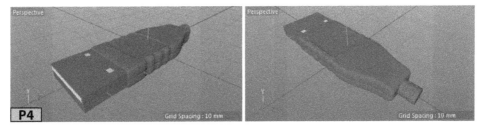

Hint Test - 2

*Set **Units** to **Millimeters**. Create a **Box** and then set its **Size X**, **Size Y**, and **Size Z** to 15, 5, and 30, respectively. Now, use various modeling tools and functions to create the USB connector model.*

Test 3: Creating a Kitchen Cabinet

Create the kitchen cabinet model [see Figure P5] using the **Cube** primitive. Use dimensions of your choice.

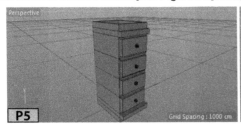 

Summary

This unit covered the following topics:

- Polygons components
- Polygon modeling techniques
- Selection tools
- Polygons structure tools
- Splines structure tools
- Modeling Objects
- Deformers

Unit CBEM1: Bonus Hands-on Exercises [Modeling]

Before you start the hands-on exercises, let's first create a project folder that will host the exercise files. Open the **Windows Explorer** and navigate to the folder where you want to save the files. Create a sub-folder with the name **unit-cbm1**.

Exercise 1: Creating an Exterior Scene

In this exercise, you will model an exterior scene using various modeling techniques [see Figure E1].

The following table summarizes the exercise:

Table E1: Creating an Exterior Scene	
Skill level	Beginner
Time to complete	90 Minutes
Topics in the section	• Getting Started • Creating the Scene
Project Folder	unit-cbme1
Units	Meter
Final exercise file	ucbme1-hoe1-end.c4d

Getting Started

Start a new scene in CINEMA 4D and set units to **Meters**.

Creating the Scene

Choose **Cube** from **SP | Object CG** to create a cube in the editor view. In **AM | Cube | Object** PG, set **Size X** to **20**, **Size Y** to **8**, and **Size Z** to **60**. Press **NB** to enable the **Gouraud Shading (Lines)** mode.

Create another Cube object and then **AM | Cube | Object** PG, set **Size X** to **14**, **Size Y** to **8**, and **Size Z** to **52**. Also, set **Segments X**, **Segments Y**, and **Segments Z** to **4**, **1**, and **14**, respectively. Now, align the **Cube.1** to the bottom of **Cube** [see Figure E2]. Choose **Filter | Grid** from the **MEV** menu to turn off the grid. Select **Cube** in the **OM** and then press **C** to make it editable. Similarly, make **Cube.1** editable. Select **Cube** in **OM** and activate the **Edges** mode from **TP**.

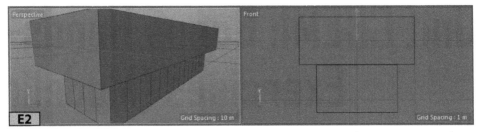

Press **MK** to enable the **Knife** tool. In **AM | Knife** PG, select **Loop** from the **Mode** drop-down and then create an edge loop, see Figure E3. Now, select the front polygons, see Figure E4, and then press **MW** to select the **Extrude Inner** tool and then in **AM | Extrude Inner | Options** PG, turn off the **Preserve Groups** switch and then set **Offset** to **0.6**, see Figure E4. Press **MT** to enable the **Extrude** tool and then in **AM | Extrude | Options** PG, set **Offset** to **-5**, see Figure E5.

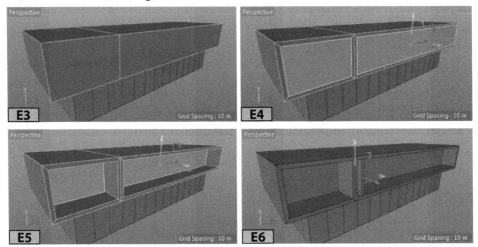

Choose **Cube** from **SP | Object CG** to create a cube in the editor view. In **AM | Cube | Object** PG, set **Size X** to **4.61**, **Size Y** to **6.827**, and **Size Z** to **0.602**. Align the cube, see Figure E6. Make sure **Cube.2** is selected in the **OM** and then choose **Arrange Objects | Duplicate** from the **Tools** menu. In **AM | Duplicate | Duplicate** PG, set **Copies** to **40**, and **Clone Mode** to **Instances**. From the **Options** PG, set **Mode** to **Linear** and then in the **Options** PG | **Position** section, set **Move XYZ** to **0, 0**, and **1.1**, respectively, see Figure E7. Select **Cube.1** in the **OM** and then select the polygon shown in Figure E8.

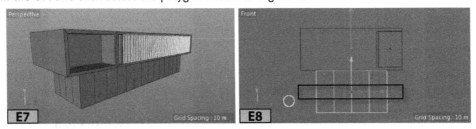

Press **MW** to select the **Extrude Inner** tool and then in **AM | Extrude Inner | Options** PG, turn off the **Preserve Groups** switch and then set **Offset** to **0.22**. Press **MT** to enable the **Extrude** tool and then in **AM | Extrude | Options** PG, set **Offset** to **-0.25**, see Figure E9. Ensure polygons are still selected and then choose **Set Selection** from the **Select** menu to create a selection set. In **AM | Basic Properties** section, **glassSelection** in the **Name** field to name the selection.

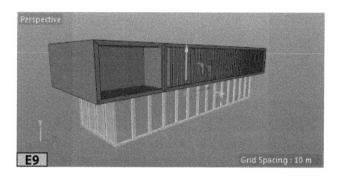

What just happened?

*Here, I've set or freeze the polygon selection. You can also set the point and edge selection. When you create a selection set, you can recall that selection later. For example, while texturing, if you want to apply glass texture to these polygons, you can easily recall the selection by double-clicking on the selection tag in the **Object Manager**. You can freeze more than **10** selections per object, however, many of the commands operate on the first **10** sets only.*

Choose **Plane** from **SP | Object** CG to create a plane in the editor view that will act as ground. In **AM | Plane | Object** PG, set **Width** to **600** and **Height** to **800**, and then align it as shown in Figure E10. Choose **Cube** from **SP | Object CG** to create a cube in the editor view. In **AM | Cube.3 | Object** PG, set **Size X** to **36**, **Size Y** to **0.2**, and **Size Z** to **71**. Now, align it with plane, see Figure E11.

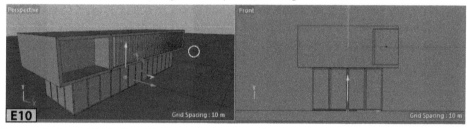

Choose **Rectangle** from **SP | Spline** CG to create a rectangle in the editor view. In **AM | Rectangle | Object** PG, set **Width** and **Height** to **12** and **48**, respectively. Turn on the **Rounding** switch and then set **Radius** to **4** and **Plane** to **XZ**. Ensure **Rectangle** is selected in **OM** and then choose **Extrude** from **SP | Generator** CG with **Alt** held down. In **AM | Extrude | Object** CG, set **Movement** XYZ to **0**, **0.4**, and **0**, respectively. Now, align object with the ground plane, see Figure E12.

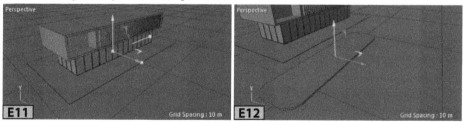

Now, we will create the light pole. Choose **Circle** from **SP | Spline** CG to create a circle in the editor view. In **AM | Object** PG, set **Radius** to **0.5** and **Plane** to **XZ**. Now, align it, as shown in Figure E13. Create three more copies of the **Circle** and set Radius to **0.4**, **0.3**, and **0.2**, respectively. Align the circles, as shown in Figure E14.

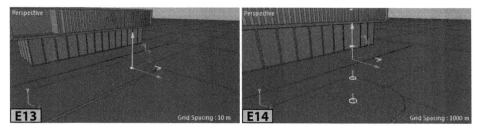

Choose **Loft** from the **Generator** CG. In **OM**, drag all circle objects onto it to make them children of the **Loft** object, the pole geometry is created in the viewport, see Figure E15. Choose **Cylinder** from **SP | Object** CG. In **AM | Cylinder | Object** PG, set **Radius** to **0.1**, **Height** to **3.168**, **Height Segments** to **1**, and then align it with the pole, see Figure E16.

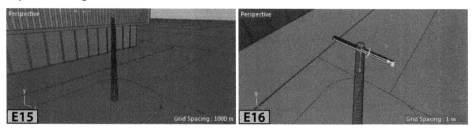

Now, we will create lights. Choose **Cube** from **SP | Object CG** to create a cube in the editor view. In **AM | Cube.4 | Object** PG, set **Size X** to **1.39**, **Size Y** to **0.71**, and **Size Z** to **0.931**. Press **C** to make **Cube.4** editable. Select the points, as shown in Figure E17 and then move them down, see Figure E18.

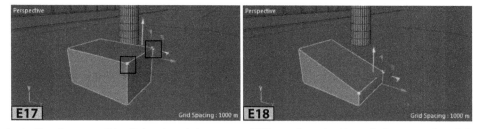

Now, select all polygons of the **Cube.4** and then press **MW** to select the **Extrude Inner** tool and then in **AM | Extrude Inner | Options** PG, turn off the **Preserve Groups** switch and then set **Offset** to **0.04**. Press UI to invert the selection and then press **MT** to enable the **Extrude** tool and then in **AM | Extrude | Options** PG, turn on the **Preserve Groups** switch. Set **Offset** to **0.018** and Maximum Angle to 180, see Figure E19.

Ensure polygons are still selected and then choose **Set Selection** from the **Select** menu to create a selection set. In **AM | Basic Properties** section, **lightCover** in the **Name** field to name the selection. Align **Cube.4** with the pole, refer Figure E20.

Create a copy of **Cube.4** and align it with the other side of the pole, see Figure E20. Now, select the **Loft**, **Cylinder**, **Cube.4**, and **Cube.5** objects in OM and press Alt+G to group the objects. Rename **Null** as **Pole.1** in OM. Make a duplicate of **Pole.1** and then rename it as **Pole.2**. Align **Pole.2**, as shown in Figure E21. Now, create main door of the building using **Box** and **Torus** primitives, see Figure E22. Now, let's create the logo of the company. Choose **Text** from **SP | Spline** CG to create a Text object in the editor view. In **AM | Text | Object** PG, set **Text** to **My Inc**. Choose a font of your choice from the **Font** drop-down. Set **Height** to **3**. You might have to adjust the height as per the font you have chosen. Align text, as shown in Figure E23.

Ensure **Text** is selected in **OM** and then choose **Extrude** from **SP | Generator** CG with **Alt** held down. In **AM | Extrude | Object** CG, set **Movement** XYZ to **0**, **0**, and **0.3**, respectively. In the **Caps** PG, select **Fillet Cap** from the **Start** and **End** drop-downs. Set **Start Steps/Radius** to **3** and **0.05** and **End Steps/Radius** to **2** and **0.02**. Set **Fillet Type** to **Engraved**, see Figure E24.

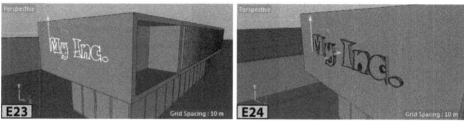

Exercise 2: Creating a Chair

In this exercises, you will create model of a chair, as shown in Figure E1.

The following table summarizes the exercise:

Table E2: Creating a Chair	
Skill level	Beginner
Time to complete	30 Minutes
Topics in the section	• Getting Started • Creating the Chair
Project Folder	unit-cbme1
Units	Inches
Final exercise file	ucbme1-hoe2-end.c4d

Getting Started

Start a new scene in CINEMA 4D and set units to **Inches**.

Creating the Chair

Choose **Pen** from **SP | Spline** CG to create a shape in the **Front** view [see Figure E2]. Select the point, as shown in Figure E3.

On **CM**, enter **9.886, 0.086**, and **-10.75** in the **X, Y**, and **Z** fields of the **Position** parameter, respectively. Similarly, set the other points using the values shown in Table E2.1.

Table E2.1 - Coordinates for creating points			
Point	**X**	**Y**	**Z**
Ist	9.886	0.086	-10.75
2nd	-9.886	0.086	-10.75
3rd	-9.886	14.834	-10.75
4th	6.285	14.834	-10.75
5th	9.886	27.011	-10.75

After entering the values, the spline is shown in Figure E4. Choose **Circle** from the **SP | Spline** CG to create a circle in the editor view. In **AM | Circle | Object** PG, set **Radius** to **0.4**. Make sure **Spline** is selected in the **OM** and then create a copy of it by **Ctrl** dragging it in the editor view about **21** units along the **Z** axis [see Figure E5]. Choose **Pen** from **SP | Spline** CG and then connect the two splines [see Figure E6].

Select the points shown in Figure E7. RMB click and choose **Chamfer** from the popup menu. Chamfer the points [see Figure E8]. Now, using the **Circle** and **Sweep** generator, create the frame of the chair [see Figure E9]. Rename **Sweep** as **Frame** in the **OM**. Create caps for frame using the **Tube** primitive [see Figure

E10]. Select all object in **OM** and then press **Alt+G** to group them. Rename the group as **frameGrp**. Now, we'll create seat for the chair.

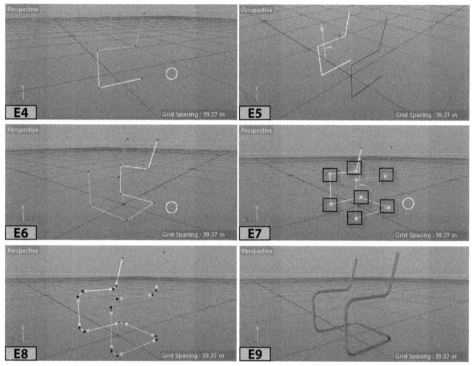

Choose **Cube** from **SP | Object CG** to create a cube in the editor view. In **AM | Cube | Object** PG, set **Size X** to **14.152**, **Size Y** to **2.5 in**, and **Size Z** to **24.283**, respectively. Also, set the **Segment X**, **Segment Y**, and **Segment Z** to **4**, **3**, and **4**, respectively. Align the **Cube** with the frame [see Figure E11].

Add a **Subdivision Surface** generator to the **Cube** to smooth it. Now, press **C** to make the **Subdivision Surface** generator editable. Rename the object as **Seat** in **OM**. Now, we'll create piping on the seat. Using the **Loop Selection** tool, select two edges as shown in Figure E12.

Choose **Commands | Edge to Spline** from the **Mesh** menu to create spline from the selected edges. Select **Seat.Spline** in **OM** and drag it out of the **Seat** group to the top level [see Figure E13]. Create a copy of the **Circle** that you we created earlier and then set its **Radius** to **0.1**. Create piping geometry by using the **Sweep** generator [see Figure E14]. Use the commands available in the **Mesh | Conversion** menu to connect the elements and to make a single editable object for the seat and piping. Rename the object as **Seat** in **OM** [see Figure E15]. Make sure seat is selected in **OM** and then choose **Axis Center | Center Axis to** from the **Mesh** menu.

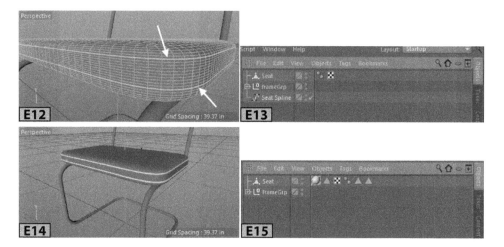

Add a **FFD** modifier to the seat. Select the middle points of **FFD** and then move them along the negative **Y** axis to create a bend in the seat [see Figure E16]. Convert seat to a single object using the **Current State to Object** command.

To make the back support of the chair, create a copy of the seat and then align it with the frame. If required, scale down the height of the back support [see Figure E17]. Select everything in **OM** and then group the object as **Chair**.

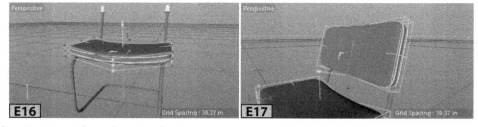

Exercise 3: Creating the Apple Logo
In this exercises, you will create 3D apple logo, as shown in Figure E1.

The following table summarizes the exercise:

Table E3 - Creating the Apple Logo	
Skill level	Beginner
Time to complete	40 Minutes
Topics in the section	• Getting Started • Creating the Logo
Project Folder	unit-cbme1
Units	Centimeters
Final exercise file	ucbme1-hoe3-end.c4d

Getting Started

Start a new scene in CINEMA 4D and set units to **Centimeters**. Maximize the **Front** viewport and then press **Shift+V** to open the viewport settings. On **AM | Back** PG, assign **apple-logo.jpg** to the **Image** parameter. Also, set **Offset X**, **Offset Y**, and **Transparency** to **8**, **398**, and **90**, respectively.

Creating the Logo

Create a shape using the **Pen** tool in the **Front** view [see Figure E2]. Make sure that the **X** coordinate value of the two end points is **0**.

Press **Ctrl+A** to select all points and then choose **Transform Tools | Mirror** from the **Mesh** menu. Click drag towards the left in **Front** view; a line appears in the view. Snap the line to the two end vertices [see Figure E3] and then release the mouse button to create the mirror copy [see Figure E4]. Select the top points [see Figure E5], RMB click and then choose **Soft Interpolation** from the popup menu. Weld the two points using the **Weld** command.

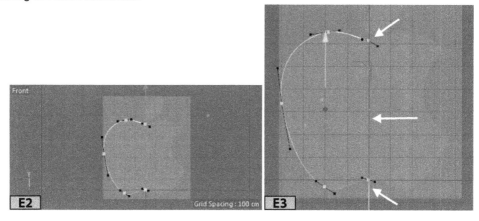

Zoom in on the bottom points [see Figure E6]. RMB click and then choose **Hard Interpolation** from the popup menu. Select **Spline** in **OM** and then from **AM | Object** PG, turn on the **Close Spline** switch. Delete the point marked with arrow in Figure E7. Now, select the remaining point, RMB click and then choose **Soft Interpolation** from the popup menu.

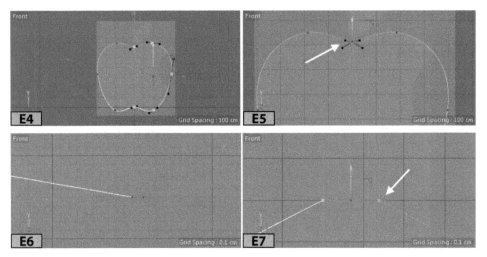

Create a **Circle** object, align it with the **Spline** [see Figure E8] and then press **C** to make it editable. On **OM**, select **Circle** and then select **Spline** [select them in the correct order]. Choose **Spline | Spline Subtract** from the **Mesh** menu to create the shape shown in Figure E9. Create two circles, make them editable and then align, as shown in Figure E10. Select the two circles and then choose **Spline | Spline And** from the **Mesh** menu to create the shape shown in Figure E11.

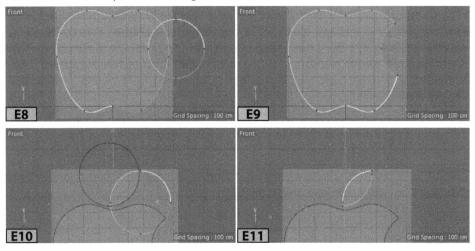

Select both splines in **OM** and then choose **Conversion | Connect Objects + Delete** from the **Mesh** menu to combine them. Now, connect the unified spline with the **Extrude** generator. On **AM | Object** PG, set **Movement** Z to **30**. On the **Caps** PG, set **Start** and **End** to **Fillet** Cap. Also, set **Step** and **Radius** for **Start** and **End** to **3** and **1.5**, respectively.

Exercise 4: Creating a Bottle

In this exercise, you will create a bottle using the **Loft** generator [see Figure E1].

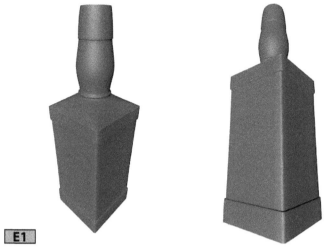

E1

The following table summarizes the exercise:

Table E4 - Creating the Bottle	
Skill level	Beginner
Time to complete	40 Minutes
Topics in the section	• Getting Started • Creating the Bottle
Project Folder	unit-cbme1
Units	Centimeters
Final exercise file	ucbme1-hoe4-end.c4d

Getting Started

Start a new scene in CINEMA 4D and set units to **Centimeters**. Maximize the **Front** viewport and then press **Shift+V** to open the viewport settings. On **AM | Back** PG, assign **whiskey.jpg** to the **Image** parameter. Also, set **Offset X**, **Offset Y**, and **Transparency** to **0**, **381**, and **90**, respectively.

Creating the Bottle

Choose **Rectangle** from **SP | Spline** CG to create a rectangle in the editor view. In **AM | Rectangle | Object** PG, set **Width** and **Height** to **232** and **232**, respectively. Turn on the **Rounding** switch and then set **Radius** to **8.248** and **Plane** to **XZ**. Align the rectangle in the **Front** view [see Figure E2]. Create a copy of the rectangle and align it [see Figure E3].

Similarly, create four more rectangles and align them [see Figure E4]. You need to adjust the size of the rectangles to get the shape you are looking for. The following table summarizes the size of the rectangles:

Table E4.1 - Size of the rectangles

Rectangle	Size [Width/Height]
Rectangle	232/232
Rectangle.1	232/232
Rectangle.2	225/225
Rectangle.3	225/225
Rectangle.4	232/232
Rectangle.5	232/232
Rectangle.6	232/232

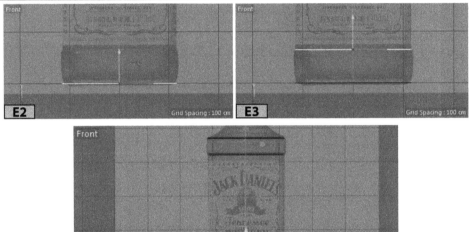

Choose **Circle** from **SP | Spline** CG to create a circle in the editor view. In **AM | Circle | Object** PG, set **Radius** to **54** and then align it [see Figure E5]. Similarly, create more circles, adjust their radii and then align them [see Figure E6]. The following table summarizes the radius of the circles:

Table E4.2 - Radius of the circles

Circle	Radius
Circle	54
Circle.1	56
Circle.2	51
Circle.3	61
Circle.4	50
Circle.5	52
Circle.6	47
Circle.7	43

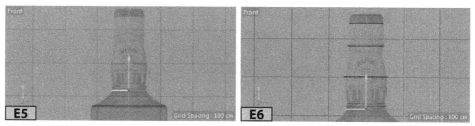

Figure E7 shows all the rectangles and circles in the scene. Now, connect all shapes with the **Loft** generator to create shape of the bottle. Ensure the order of the shapes is as shown in Figure E8.

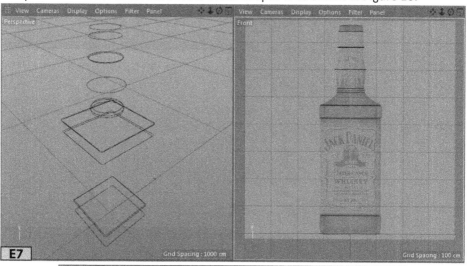

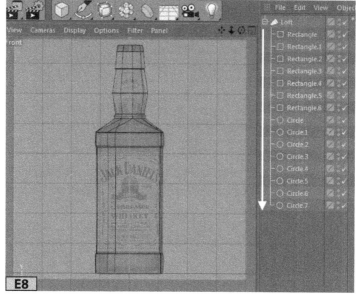

Exercise 5: Creating a Chair

In this exercise, you will create a chair using the spline and polygon modeling techniques [see Figure E1].

E1

The following table summarizes the exercise:

Table E5 - Creating the Chair	
Skill level	Beginner
Time to complete	45 Minutes
Topics in the section	• Getting Started • Creating Chair
Project Folder	unit-cbme1
Units	Inches
Final exercise file	ucbme1-hoe5-end.c4d

Getting Started

Start a new scene in CINEMA 4D and set units to **Inches**.

Creating the Chair

We'll first create a cube that will work like a template that will help us in the modeling process. Choose **Cube** from **SP | Object CG** to create a cube in the editor view. In **AM | Cube | Object** PG, set **Size X** to **20**, **Size Y** to **30**, and **Size Z** to **20**. Also, set **Segment X**, **Segment Y**, and **Segment Z** to **1**, **2**, and **4**, respectively. Press **O** to frame the object in the editor view. Press **NB** to enable the **Gouraud Shading (Lines)** mode, see Figure E2.

Press **Shift+S** to enable snapping and then choose **Pen** from **SP**. Now, create a rectangular spline by clicking on the four corners of the lower half of the cube [see Figure E3].

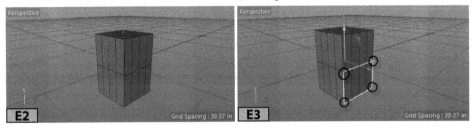

Move the spline slightly to the right of the cube so that it is visible clearly. Select the two top points and then chamfer them using the **Chamfer** tool [see Figure E4]. Also, chamfer the bottom points [see Figure E5]. Create a circle of radius **0.3** and then create the frame of the chair using the **Sweep** modifier [see Figure E6]. Create a cube and then set its **Size X** to **2.6**, **Size Y** to **1**, and **Size Z** to **1.5**. Also, turn on the **Fillet** switch and then set **Fillet Radius** to **0.3**. Align, it with the bottom of the frame [see Figure E7]. Create copy of the cube and then align it as shown in Figure E7.

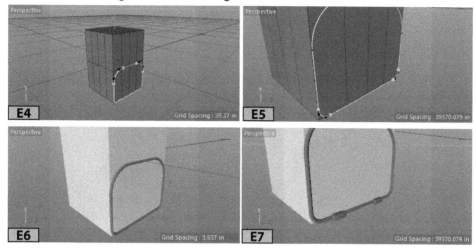

Select everything in **OM** except **Cube** and then press **Alt+G** to group the objects. Rename the group as **Frame.1**. Create a copy of the **Frame.1** and align it with the other side of the **Cube** [see Figure E8]. Hide **Cube**.

Now, we will create the seat and back support. Create a plane and then in **AM**, set **Width**, **Height**, **Width Segments**, and **Height Segments** to **23**, **20**, **1**, and **1**, respectively. Align the plane with the frame [see Figure E9]. Make the plane editable by pressing **C**. Select the edge [see Figure E10] and then drag it upward about **15** units with the **Ctrl** held down to create the back support [see Figure E10]. Similarly, extrude the front edge using **Ctrl** [see Figure E11].

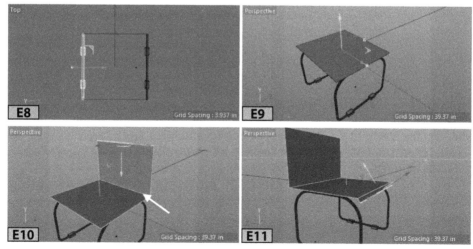

Select the edge [see Figure E12] and then bevel it using the **Bevel** tool [see Figure E13]. Use the value **1** for **Offset** and **3** for **Subdivision** in **AM | Bevel | Tool Option** PG. Create edge loops using the **Knife** tool [see Figure E14]. Select the edge ring, as shown in Figure E15 and then press **Alt+X** three times to connect the edges [see Figure E16]. Select all polygons of the **Plane** and then extrude them by **0.169** units using the **Extrude** tool [see Figure E17].

Now, you need to create a bend in the seat and back support using the **FFD** modifier. Finally, add a **Subdivision Surface** generator to smooth the chair [see Figure E18].

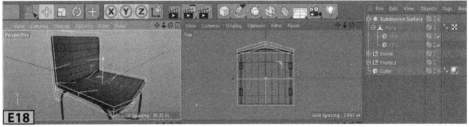

Delete **Cube** from the scene. In the **OM**, select all objects and press **Alt+G** to group them. Rename the group as **Chair**. Connect an **Array** object with **Chair**. In **AM | Array Object | Object** PG, set **Radius** and **Copies** parameters as required.

Exercise 6: Creating a Flask

In this exercise, you will create a flask using the spline and polygon modeling techniques [see Figure E1].

The following table summarizes the exercise:

Table E5 - Creating the Flask	
Skill level	Beginner
Time to complete	30 Minutes
Topics in the section	• Getting Started • Creating Flask
Project Folder	unit-cbme1
Units	Inches
Final exercise file	ucbme1-hoe6-end.c4d

Getting Started

Start a new scene in CINEMA 4D and set units to **Inches**.

Creating the Flask

Create basic shape of the flask [see Figure E2] using circles and the **Loft** generator, as done in Exercise 4. The following table summarizes the radius of the circles:

Table E6.1 - Radius of the circles	
Circle	**Radius**
Circle	18
Circle.1	18
Circle.2	17
Circle.3	17
Circle.4	12

Choose **Tube** from **SP | Object CG** to create a tube in the editor view. On **AM | Tube | Object** PG, set **Inner Radius** to **12**, **Outer Radius** to **13**, **Rotation Segments** to **24**, and **Height** to **12**. Align it with the flask's lower body [see Figure E3]. Make the tube editable and then move the points to get the shape, as shown in Figure E4. Press **UO** to optimize the tube model.

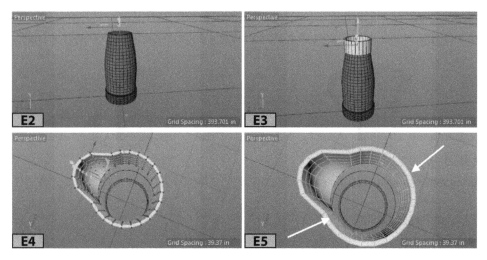

Select the edge loops [see Figure E5] and then bevel them [see Figure E6]. Select the polygons [see Figure E7].

Press **UC** to collapse them. Now create a circular loop using the **Polygon Pen** tool [see Figure E8]. Select the polygons shown in Figure E9, and then inner extrude them [see Figure E10]. Now, extrude the newly created polygons [see Figure E11].

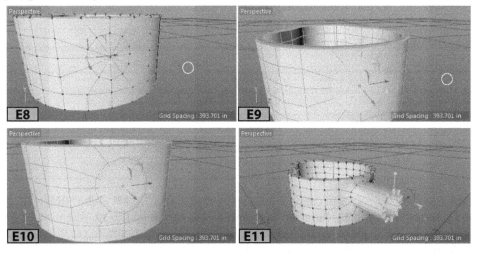

Connect **Tube** with the **Subdivision Surface** generator. Create a cylinder and align it with the tube [see Figure E12].

To create handle, create a **Tube** object, apply **Taper** and **Bend** deformers to it and then align with the flask [see Figure E13].

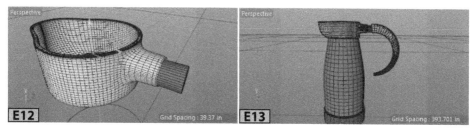

Now, create the cap using the **Sphere** object [see Figure E14].

This page intentionally left blank

Index

This page intentionally left blank

Other Books Published by Rising Polygon

Rising Polygon Publishing

[Best Textbooks at Lower Prices]

Modeling Techniques

with

3ds Max 2016 and CINEMA 4D R17 Studio

The Ultimate Beginner's Guide

@risingpolygon
www.risingpolygon.ca

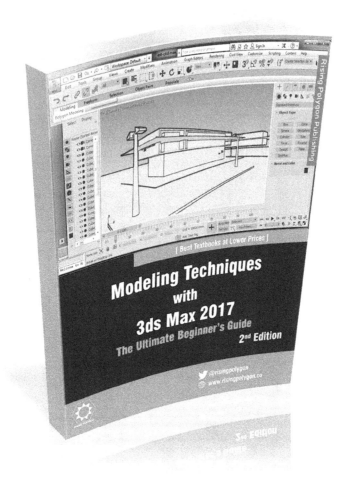

[Best Textbooks at Lower Prices]

Modeling Techniques
with
3ds Max 2017
The Ultimate Beginner's Guide

2nd Edition

@risingpolygon
www.risingpolygon.co

Modeling Techniques
with
CINEMA 4D R17 Studio
The Ultimate Beginner's Guide
2nd Edition

[Best Textbooks at Lower Prices]

Modeling Techniques
with
3ds Max 2017 and CINEMA 4D R17 Studio
The Ultimate Beginner's Guide
2nd Edition

@risingpolygon
www.risingpolygon.co

Rising Polygon Publishing

Rising Polygon Publishing

| Best Textbooks at Lower Prices |

Getting Started with
General Materials
In 3ds Max 2017

@risingpolygon
www.risingpolygon.co

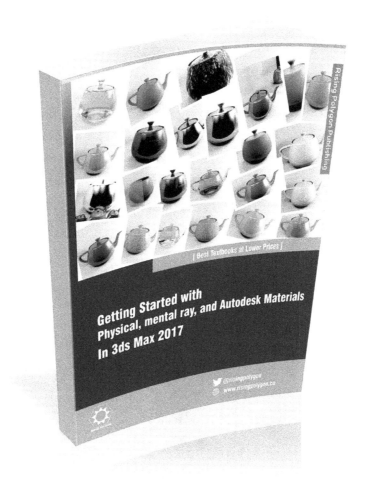

Getting Started with
Physical, mental ray, and Autodesk Materials
In 3ds Max 2017

[Best Textbooks at Lower Prices]

Modeling and Texturing Techniques

With

3ds Max 2017

The Ultimate Beginner's Guide

* Contains 3 bonus chapters on creating cutsom maps and textures using Photoshop.

🐦 @risingpolygon
🌐 www.risingpolygon.co

Rising Polygon Publishing

www.ingramcontent.com/pod-product-compliance
Lightning Source LLC
Chambersburg PA
CBHW060147060326
40690CB00018B/4012